THE OPEN CONSPIRACY

BLUE PRINTS FOR A WORLD REVOLUTION

by

H. G. Wells

Albatross Publishers
Naples, Italy
2017

Originally Published in London Victor Gollancz 1928

ISBN 978-1-946963-03-1

©2017 *Albatross Publishers*

H. G. WELLS

THE OPEN CONSPIRACY

BLUE PRINTS
FOR A WORLD REVOLUTION

LONDON

VICTOR GOLLANCZ LTD

14 Henrietta Street Covent Garden

1928

To

DANIEL GERBAULT

who asked me to

write this book

CONTENTS

PREFACE

This book states as plainly and clearly as possible the essential ideas of my life, the perspective of my world. Everything else that I have been or done seems to me to have been contributory to or illustrative of these ideas and suggestions. My other writings, with hardly an exception, explore, try over, illuminate, comment upon or flower out of the essential matter that I here attempt at last to strip bare to its foundations and state unmistakably. This is my religion. Here are my directive aims and the criteria of all I do.

Since the subject of this book is the whole destiny of man, and the whole duty of man, it will certainly be called a pretentious book. That will be a charge too obvious to miss and we can consider it made. But it is no more pretentious to work upon the whole of life than upon parts and aspects of life ; it is a question of scale and method ; the intellectual effort needed, the quality of the work required for making the map of a continent may be less than and inferior to that demanded by the chemical examination of a muscle fibre or the investigation of atomic structure. A man is not pretentious because he works with the theodolite instead of the microscope. Some men work upon the bulkier common issues ; some upon finer and subtler questions. To every man his task. There is no hierarchy in human thought.

Here, given tentatively, with many evident faults and gaps, is a scheme for all human conduct. It discusses what should man be doing and what should men be doing. It states a general form and direction for the crowding rush of modern ideas and impulsions. I believe that upon such lines as I have drawn, the creative forces in our species can be organised and may be organised, in a comprehensive fight against individual and collective frustration and death. I believe also that there is no other direction but this direction along which mankind can escape from the insecurity of an animal which has been evolved and which may presently be degraded or extinguished in the play of material things. The accident of a great opportunity, I hold, has happened to our kind. It is opportunity and not destiny we face.

So I bear my witness and argue my design. This is, I declare, the truth and the way of salvation. If I could, I would put this book before every mind in the world. I would say, tell me where this is wrong, or tell me why you do not live after these principles.

I pray the reader for a patient reading. This is, I submit, matter of very great moment to him. My phrasing, my idiom of thought may not be his. Will he forgive that for the sake of the substance I am putting before him ? It is astir already in many intelligences and it is an amplifying group of ideas. I am merely the observer who notes his own adhesion and draws attention, eagerly and earnestly, to what is going on and to the quality of our present occasion. Will the reader at least try to understand before he refutes ? I am discussing here the

possibility of an immense and hopeful revolution
in human affairs and of an enlivening and en-
nobling change in our lives. I am discussing
whether our species, he and I with it and part of
it, is to live or die.

CHAPTER I

NECESSITY OF RELIGION TO HUMAN LIFE

Few people, if any, are always sustained by un-
selfish or religious motives, and few or none are
altogether beyond their influence. The daily lives
of the great majority of human beings are frankly
irreligious ; they seem to differ only in their scope,
variety and intelligence from the lives of animals ;
they are determined by instinctive impulses, individual desires and personal ends ; they pass from
one satisfaction or disappointment to another ; they
are attracted and deflected by casual encounters ;
they forget more or less completely and they resume.
Nevertheless, the conduct of most lives is restricted
and defined by the prevalent conceptions of what is
honourable and becoming, and right and wrong.
Although the lives of the great run of people are
neither moral essentially nor essentially religious,
they respect current moral and religious forms and
maxims, just as they conform to current usages and
beaten tracks. It is the line of least resistance for
them, and that suffices.

Communities have been held together in the past
and are still held together by laws and moral codes
systematised upon religious ideas, and this although
few people have more than a superficial apprehension of such ideas. Religion in its completeness has

always been the peculiarity of a minority; it has shaped and innervated communities but never pervaded them throughout. But its presence seems to have been necessary for collective life. Without it morality was baseless and law unjustifiable. The intermittent disposition of most human beings towards some sort of righteousness beyond self-seeking has been upheld, as some sprawling, weak-jointed climbing plant may be upheld on a trellis, by that more steadfast minority of sincere and devoted persons. It is these latter who have preserved disinterested standards, and who still preserve them; who have been and who continue to be the salt of the earth.

Religious ideas in the past have derived from the most diverse emotional and intellectual origins in the integrating mind of man. Speculative explanations, metaphors hardened by usage into quasi-factual statements, fantasies arising out of germinating and suppressed impulses, false analogies, parables begotten and lit by flashes of spiritual insight, traditions misconceived and distorted, dogmatic excesses in explicitness evoked by the irritation of contradictory criticism, the odd compromises of theological diplomatists, the craving for supernatural sanctions and vindications and the nightmare creations of fear, that haunting shadow of all conscious life, have mingled inextricably in every religious fabric. But the survival value of a religion to a community has lain always in the practical assistance it afforded in the subordination of self and the achievement of co-operative loyalties not otherwise obtainable. No community seems ever to have been held together in wholesome and vigorous collective life by " enlightened self-interest " alone. Enlightened self-interest in exceptional cases and under slight or moderate stresses may produce enough simulated disinterestedness to be practically undistinguish-able from public virtue, and the great mass of lives in every community is no doubt kept at this or that moral level, and in this or that form of behaviour according to the quality and intensity of the beliefs that hold that community together with little or no co-operating force in the lives themselves. But some-where and effectively in that community the sus-taining beliefs of the community must be passionately and sincerely held and maintained. A community where binding beliefs have decayed altogether is like a building whose mortar has been changed to sand. It may stand for a time, but it stands precariously.

Now in the communities in which we are living to-day there has been a far-reaching weakening and change in religious beliefs. This has been due to an enormous growth of knowledge, to an enhanced vigour of criticism, to a relative enfeeblement of government and authority which released unpre-cedented freedoms of speech and permitted the crystallisation of doubts into coherent and militant denials. At the same time there have been develop-ments of the mechanical conditions of life that have enlarged the scale of possible human operations, made economical life increasingly international and brought once autonomous states and regions into a mutually disintegrative intimacy of reaction. The stresses upon our communities are greater than they have ever been and the binding forces less. The outlook before our race seems therefore to be wider, more uncertain and much more dangerous than has ever appeared before.

In the past, in the history of every community there have been phases of moral and religious confusion. The beliefs and ideas of right conduct that have served hitherto begin, in the presence of new circumstances or new challenges, to lose authority or to fail in meeting current moral problems. An age of relaxation and a sort of experimental wickedness dawns. Scruples vanish. Treachery, cruelty, unrestrained self-indulgence, which have been kept under hatches, emerge conspicuously. Government becomes more adventurous, tyrannous and unjust, and the moral distinction between ruler and brigand fines away to the vanishing-point. There seems no longer any good faith nor any sweetness of soul in human life, except among the sacrificial simple. What will for a better life still manifests itself in the world is for a while quite unable to take hold of the disorder. Italy in the Machiavellian period and Germany after the intricate wars of the Reformation may be cited as typical instances of such " wicked " phases in social history. Yet it was not that the heart of man changed for the worse in those ages, not that there was a sudden generation of vipers, but that intellectual confusion had divided and enfeebled that graver-spirited minority which had, under more assured conditions, sustained the faith of most people and the moral disciplines of everyone. The quality of the ingredients of the human mixture remained the same, but the restraining and directive forces had in their interplay come upon a phase of mutual neutralisation and collective ineffectiveness.

There are many signs that to-day over large parts of the world there is a drift towards such another disintegrative and distressful phase. The brigand, the boss and the adventurer become portentously successful and immune. People who, in other times, would have been active and confident in their own lives and vigorously co-operative in the control of human affairs are uncertain in their hearts and un-happy in their interventions. The old faiths have become unconvincing, unsubstantial and insincere, and though there are clear intimations of a new faith in the world, it still awaits embodiment in formulæ and organisations that will bring it into effective reaction upon human affairs as a whole.

This present essay is an attempt to assemble these intimations in a form that will be available for the practical direction of the writer's and the reader's life.

CHAPTER II

SUBORDINATION OF SELF THE ESSENCE OF RELIGION

The religions that hitherto have served over wide regions and for considerable periods of time to sustain men in more or less orderly, honest, decent and progressive societies, have been presented to the generality and accepted by the generality in extremely attenuated forms. In their beginnings they were all intense and uncompromising. Christianity, for example, began with the completest communism, Buddhism with an entire renunciation of earthly desire, Islam with the passionate and forcible dedication of the whole world to Allah. Sooner or later, however, the propagandist came to terms with human weakness and struck a bargain for a cheaper form of common proselyte.

But though the creed and practice might need lightening and fitting to customary humanity before they could be universally accepted, there appeared no essential conflict in the process between the intense and the superficial form. The common man assented to everything in the doctrine, and merely asked to have the more difficult and onerous terms deferred or mitigated. His plea for his personal insufficiency was weakness and not dissent.

In their completeness, in their esoteric forms, in the life that was professionally *religious*, religions have always demanded great subordinations of self. Therein lay their creative usefulness. There is no such thing as a self-contained religion, a private religious solo Certain forms of Protestantism and some mystical types come near to making religion a secluded duet between the individual and his divinity, but here that may be regarded as a perversion of the religious impulse. Just as the normal sexual complex excites and stirs the individual out of his egotism to serve the ends of the race, so the normal religious process takes the individual out of his egotism for the service of the community. It is not a bargain, a "social contract," between the individual and the community ; it is a subordination of both the existing individual and the existing community in relation to something, a divinity, a divine order, a standard, a righteousness, more important than either. What is called in the phraseology of certain religions "conviction of sin" and "the flight from the City of Destruction" are familiar instances of this reference of the self-centred individual and the current social life to something far better than either the one or the other.

This is the third element in the religious relationship, a hope, a promise, an objective which turns the convert not only from himself but from the "world" as it is, towards better things. First comes self-disregard, then service, and then this reconstructive creative urgency.

For that minority of minds which I have already spoken of as the salt of the earth, this aspect of religion seems to have been its primary attraction. One has to remember that there is a will for religion

Bc

scattered throughout mankind. Religion has never
pursued its distinctive votaries ; they have come to
meet it. The desire to give oneself to greater ends
than the everyday life affords, and to give oneself
freely, is clearly dominant in that minority and
traceable in an incalculable proportion of the
majority.

CHAPTER III

NEED FOR A RESTATEMENT OF RELIGION

Every great religion has explained itself in the form of a history and a cosmogony. It has been felt necessary to say *Why* and *To what end*. Every religion has had necessarily to adopt the physical conceptions and usually also to assume many of the moral and social values current at the time of its foundation. It could not transcend the philosophical phrases and attitudes that seemed then to supply the natural frame for a faith, nor draw upon anything beyond the store of scientific knowledge of its time. In these conditions lurked the seeds of an ultimate decay and supersession of every religion.

But as the idea of continual change going farther and farther from existing realities and never returning to them is a new one, each fresh development of religion in the world so far has been proclaimed in perfect good faith as the culminating and final truth. The suggestion of the possibility of further restatement is an unsettling suggestion ; it seems to undermine conviction and it breaks the ranks of the believers because there are enormous variations in the capacities of men to recognise the same spirit under a changing shape. While some intelligences can recognise the same God under a variety of names and symbols without any severe strain, others cannot

even detect the most contrasted Gods one from the
other, provided they wear the same mask and title.
It appears a perfectly natural and reasonable thing
to many minds to restate religion in terms of biological and psychological necessity, while to others
any variation in the phrasing of the faith seems to be
nothing less than atheistical misrepresentations of the
most damnable kind. For them God, a God still
anthropomorphic enough to have a will and purpose,
to display preferences and reciprocate emotions, to
be indeed a person, must be retained until the end of
time. For others, God can be thought of as a Great
First Cause, as impersonal and inhuman as atomic
structure.

It is because of the historical and philosophical
commitments they have undertaken, and because of
concessions made to common human weaknesses in
regard to such once apparently minor but now vital
moral issues as property, mental activity and public
veracity—rather than of any inadequacy in their
adaptation to psychological needs—that the present
discredit of recognised religions has come about.
They no longer seem even roughly truthful upon
issues of fact, and they give no imperatives over large
fields of conduct in which perplexity is prevalent.
People will say : " I could be perfectly happy leading
the life of a Catholic devotee if only I could believe."
But most of the framework of religious explanation
upon which that life is sustained is too old-fashioned
and too irrelevant to admit of that thoroughness
of belief which is necessary for the devotion of
intelligent people.

Great ingenuity has been shown by modern writers

and thinkers in the adaptation of venerated religious expressions to new ideas. *Peccavi.* The word " God " is in most minds so associated with the concept of religion that it is abandoned only with the greatest reluctance. The word remains though the idea is continually attenuated. He is pushed farther and farther from actuality and His definition becomes increasingly a bundle of negations, until at last, in His rôle of The Absolute, He becomes an entirely negative expression. While we can speak of good, say some, we can speak of God. God is the possibility of goodness, the good side of things. If phrases in which the name of God is used are to be abandoned, they argue, religion will be left speechless before many occasions.

Certainly there is something beyond the individual that is and the world that is ; on that we have already insisted as a characteristic of all religions ; that persuasion is the essence of faith and the key to courage. But whether that is to be considered, even after the most strenuous exercises in personification, as a greater person or a comprehensive person is another matter. Personality is the last vestige of anthropomorphism. The modern urge to a precise veracity is against such concessions to traditional expression. On the other hand there is in many fine religious minds a desire amounting almost to a necessity for an object of devotion so individualised as to be capable at least of a receptive consciousness even if no definite response is conceded. One type of mind can accept a reality in itself which another must project and dramatise before it can comprehend it and react to it. The human soul is an intricate thing which will not endure elucidation when that passes beyond a certain degree of harshness and roughness. The human spirit has learnt love, devotion, obedience and humility in relation to other personalities, and with difficulty it takes the final step to a transcendent subordination, from which the last shred of personality has been stripped. In matters not immediately material, language has to work by metaphors, and though every metaphor carries its own peculiar risks of confusion we cannot do without them. Great intellectual tolerance is necessary, therefore—a cultivated disposition to translate and retranslate from one metaphysical or emotional idiom to another—if there is not to be a deplorable wastage of moral force in our world.

Three profound differences between the mental dispositions of the present time and those of preceding ages have to be realised if current developments of the religious impulse are to be seen in their correct relationship to the religious life of the past. There has been a great advance in the analysis of psychic processes and the courage with which men have probed into the origins of human thought and feeling. Following upon the biological advances that have made us recognise fish and amphibian in the bodily structure of man, have come these parallel developments in which we see elemental fear and lust and self-love moulded, modified and exalted, under the stress of social progress, into intricate human motives. Our conception of sin and our treatment of sin have been profoundly modified by this analysis. Our former sins are seen as ignorances, inadequacies and bad habits, and the moral conflict is robbed of three-fourths of its ego-centred melo-dramatic quality. We are no longer moved to be less wicked ; we are moved to organise our con-ditioned reflexes and lead a life less fragmentary and silly.

Secondly, the conception of individuality has been influenced and relaxed by biological thought, so that we do not think so readily of the individual *contra mundum* as our fathers did. We begin to realise that we are egotists by misapprehension. Nature cheats the self to serve the purposes of the species by filling it with wants that war against its private interests. As our eyes are opened to these things, we see ourselves as beings greater or less than the definitive self. Man's soul is no longer his own. It is, he discovers, part of a greater being which lived before he was born and will survive him. The idea of a survival of the definite individual with all the accidents and idiosyncrasies of his temporal nature upon him, dissolves to nothing in this new view of immortality.

The third of the main contrasts between modern and former thought which have rendered the general shapes of established religion old-fashioned and un-serviceable, is a reorientation of current ideas about time. The powerful disposition of the human mind to explain everything as the inevitable unfolding of a past event which, so to speak, sweeps the future helplessly before it, has been checked by a mass of subtle criticisms. The conception of progress as a broadening and increasing purpose, a conception which is taking hold of the human imagination more

and more firmly, turns religious life towards the
future. We think no longer of submission to the
irrevocable decrees of absolute dominion, but of
participation in an adventure on behalf of a power
that gains strength and establishes itself. The
history of our world, which has been unfolded
to us by science, runs counter to all the histories
on which religions have been based. There was
no Creation in the past, we begin to realise, but
eternally there is creation ; there was no Fall to
account for the conflict of good and evil, but a
stormy ascent. Life as we know it is a mere
beginning.

It seems unavoidable that if religion is to develop
unifying and directive power in the present confusion
of human affairs it must adapt itself to this forward-
looking, individuality-analysing turn of mind ; it
must divest itself of its sacred histories, its gross pre-
occupations, its posthumous prolongation of personal
ends. The desire for service, for subordination, for
permanent effect, for an escape from the distressful
pettiness and mortality of the individual life, is the
undying element in every religious system. The time
has come to strip religion right down to that, to
strip it for greater tasks than it has ever faced before.
The histories and symbols that served our fathers
encumber and divide us. Sacraments and rituals
harbour disputes and waste our scanty emotions.
The explanation of why things are is an unnecessary
effort in religion. The essential fact in religion
is the desire for religion and not how it came
about. If you do not want religion, no persuasions,
no convictions about your place in the universe

can give it to you. The first sentence in the modern creed must be, not " I believe " but " I give myself."

To what ? And how ? To these questions we must next address ourselves.

CHAPTER IV

OBJECTIVE EXPRESSION OF MODERN RELIGION

To give oneself religiously is a continuing operation expressed in a series of acts. It can be nothing else. You cannot dedicate yourself and then go away to live just as you have lived before. It is a poor travesty of religion that does not produce an essential change in the life which embraces it. But in the established and older religions of our race, this change of conduct has involved much self-abasement merely to the God or Gods, or much self-mortification merely with a view to the moral perfecting of self. Christian devotion, for example, in these early stages, before the hermit life gave place to organised monastic life, did not to any extent direct itself to service except the spiritual service of other human beings. But as Christianity became a definite social organising force, it took on a great series of healing, comforting, helping, manufacturing and educational activities. The modern tendency has been and is all in the direction of minimising what one might call self-centred devotion and self-subjugation, and of expanding and developing external service. The idea of inner perfectibility dwindles with the diminishing importance attached to individuality. We cease to think of mortifying or exalting or perfecting ourselves and seek to lose ourselves in a greater life.

We think less and less of " conquering " self and more and more of escaping from self. If we attempt to perfect ourselves in any respect it is only as a soldier sharpens and polishes an essential weapon.

Our quickened apprehension of continuing change, our broader and fuller vision of the history of life, disabuse our minds of many limitations set to the imaginations of our predecessors. Much that they saw as fixed and determinate, we see as transitory and controllable. They saw life fixed in its species and subjected to irrevocable laws. We see life struggling insecurely but with a gathering successfulness for freedom and power against restriction and death. We see life coming at last to our tragic and hopeful human level. Certain great possibilities, certain mighty problems, we realise, confront mankind to-day. They frame our existences. The practical aspect, the material form, the embodiment, of the modernised religious impulse is the direction of the whole life to the solution of these problems and the realisation of their possibilities.

The modern religious life like all forms of religious life must needs have its own subtle and deep inner activities, its meditations, its self-confrontations, its phases of stress and search and appeal, its serene and prayerful moods, but these inward aspects do not come into the scope of this present enquiry, which is concerned entirely with the outward shape, the direction and the organisation of modern religious effort, with the question of what, given religious devotion, we have to do and how that has to be done.

Now as the modern vision of life has grown clear, certain vast possibilities and certain great dangers have become plain. They challenge mankind. They furnish an entirely new frame and setting for the moral life. In the fixed and limited outlook of the past, practical good works took the form mainly of palliative measures against evils that were conceived of as incurable ; the religious community nursed the sick, fed the hungry, provided sanctuary for the fugitive, pleaded with the powerful for mercy. It did not dream of preventing sickness, famine or tyranny. Otherworldliness was its ready refuge from the invincible evil and confusion of the existing scheme of things. It is possible now to imagine an order in human affairs from which these evils have been largely or entirely eliminated. More and more people are coming to realise that such an order is a material possibility. And with the realisation that this is a material possibility, we can no longer be content with a field of good deeds and right action restricted to palliative and consolatory activities. Such things are merely " first-aid." The religious mind grows bolder than it has ever been before. It pushes through the curtain it once imagined was a barrier. It apprehends its larger obligations. The way in which our activities conduce to the realisation of that conceivable better order in human affairs, becomes the new criterion of conduct.

The realisation of this conceivable better order involves certain necessary achievements. It is impossible for any clear-headed person to suppose that the ever more destructive stupidities of war can be eliminated from human affairs until some common political control dominates the earth, and unless certain pressures due to the growth of population, due to the enlarging scope of human operations or due to conflicting standards and traditions of life, are disposed of. To avoid the positive evils of war and to attain the new levels of prosperity and power that now come into view, an effective world control, not merely of armed force but of the production and main movements of staple commodities and the drift and expansion of population, is required. It is absurd to dream of peace and world-wide progress without that much control. These things assured, the abilities and energies of a greatly increased proportion of human beings could be diverted to the happy activities of scientific research and creative work with an ever-increasing release and enlargement of human possibility. Such a forward stride in human life, the first stride in a mighty continuing advance, an advance to which no limit appears, is now materially possible. The opportunity is offered to mankind. But there is no certainty, no material necessity, that it should ever be taken. It will not be taken by mankind inadvertently. It can only be taken through such an organisation of will and energy to take it as this world has never seen before.

These are the new conditions that unfold themselves before the more alert minds of our generation and which will presently become the general mental background, as the modern interpretations of the history of life and of material and mental possibilities establish themselves. Evil political, social and economic usages and arrangements may seem obdurate and huge, but they are neither permanent nor uncontrollable. They can be controlled, however, only by an effort more powerful and determined than the instincts and inertias that sustain them. Religion, modern and disillusioned, has for its outward task to set itself to the control and direction of political, social and economic life, or admit itself a mere drug for easing discomfort. Can it or can it not synthesise the needed effort to lift mankind out of our present disorders, dangers, baseness, frustrations and futilities, to a phase of relative security, accumulating knowledge, systematic and continuing growth in power and the widespread deep happiness of hopeful and increasing life?

Our answer here is that it can, and our subject now is to enquire what are the necessary opening stages in the synthesis of that effort. We write here for those who believe that it can, and who do already grasp the implications of world history and contemporary scientific achievement.

CHAPTER V

THE FRAME OF THE TASK
BEFORE MANKIND :
THE WORLD COMMONWEAL

Before we can consider the forms and methods of attacking their inevitable task that the serious minority of human beings must adopt, it will be well to draw the main lines and attempt some measure of the magnitude of that task. What are the new forms that it is sought to impose upon human life and how are they to be evolved from or imposed upon the current forms? And against what passive and active resistances has this to be done?

There can be no pause for replacement in the affairs of life. Day must follow day and the common activities continue. The new world as a going concern must arise out of the old as a going concern.

Now the most comprehensive conception of this new world is of one politically, socially and economically unified. Within that frame fall all the other ideas of our progressive ambition. To this end a small but increasing body of people in the world set their faces and seek to direct their lives. Still more at present apprehend it as a possibility but do not *dare* to desire it, because of the enormous difficulties that intervene and because they see as yet no intimations of a way through or round these difficulties. The great majority of human beings have still to see the human adventure as one whole ; they are obsessed by the air of permanence and finality in established things ; they accept current reality as ultimate reality. They take the world as they find it. But here we are writing for the modern-minded, and for them it is impossible to think of the world as secure and satisfactory until there exists a single world common-weal, preventing war and controlling those moral, biological and economic forces that would otherwise lead to wars.

The method of direction of such a world commonweal is not likely to imitate the methods of existing sovereign states. It will be a new sort of direction with a new psychology. There will be little need for President or King to lead the marshalled hosts of humanity, for where there is no war there is no need of any leader to lead hosts anywhere, and in a polyglot world a parliament of mankind is an inconceivable instrument of government. The fundamental organisation of contemporary states is still plainly military and that is exactly what a world organisation cannot be. Flags, uniforms, national anthems, patriotism sedulously cultivated in church and school, the brag, blare and bluster of our competing sovereignties, belong to the phase of development we would supersede. The reasonable desire of all of us is that we should have the collective affairs of the world managed by suitably equipped groups of the most interested, intelligent and devoted people and that their activities should be subjected to a free, open, watchful criticism, restrained from making spasmodic interruptions but powerful enough to modify or supersede without haste or delay whatever is weakening or unsatisfactory in the general direction.

A world movement for the supersession or enlargement or fusion of existing political, economic and social institutions, must necessarily, as it grows, draw closer and closer to questions of practical control. It is likely in its growth to incorporate many active public servants, and many industrial and financial leaders and directors. It may also assimilate great numbers of intelligent workers. As its activities spread it will work out a whole system of special methods of co-operation. It will learn as it grows and by growing the business of general direction and how to develop its critical function. So that the movement we contemplate will by its very nature be one aiming, not so much to set up a world direction as to become itself a world direction, and the educational and militant forms of its opening phase will, as experience is gained and power and responsibility acquired, evoke step by step forms of administration and research and correction.

The modernisation of the religious impulse leads us straight to the effort for the establishment of the world state as a duty, and the close consideration of the necessary organisation of that effort will bring the reader to the conclusion that a movement aiming at the establishment of a world-directorate, however restricted that movement may be at first in numbers and power, must either contemplate the prospect of

Cc

itself developing in part or as a whole into a world-directorate, and by assimilation, as a whole into a modern world community, or admit from the outset the futility, the spare-time amateurishness, of its gestures.

CHAPTER VI

BROAD CHARACTERISTICS OF THE WORLD COMMONWEAL

Continuing our examination of the practical task before the modern mind, we may next note the main lines of contemporary aspiration within this comprehensive outline of a world commonweal. Any sort of unification of human affairs will not serve the ends we seek, we aim at a particular sort of unification ; a world Cæsar is hardly better from the progressive viewpoint than world chaos ; the unity we seek must mean the liberation of human thought, experiment and creative effort. A successful conspiracy merely to seize governments and wield and retain world power would be at best only the empty frame of success, it might be the exact reverse of success. Release from the threat of war and the waste of international economic conflicts is a poor release if it demands as its price the loss of all other liberties.

It is because we desire a unification of human direction, not simply for the sake of unity, but as a means to certain definite ends, that it is necessary, at any cost—in delay, in loss of effective force, in strategic or tactical disadvantage—that the light of free, abundant criticism should play upon that unified direction and upon the movements and organisations leading to the establishment of that unified direction.

Man is an imperfect animal and never quite trustworthy in the dark. Neither morally nor intellectually is he safe from lapses. Most of us who are past our first youth know how little we can even trust ourselves, and are glad to have our activities checked and guarded by a sense of inspection. It is for this reason that a movement to realise the conceivable better state of the world, must deny itself the advantages of secret methods or tactical insincerities. It must leave that to its adversaries. We must declare our end plainly from the outset and risk no misunderstandings of our procedure.

The conspiracy of modern religion against the established institutions of the world must be an open conspiracy and cannot remain righteous otherwise. It is lost if it goes underground. Every step to world unity must be taken in the daylight, or the sort of unity that will be won will be found to be scarcely worth the winning. The essential task will have to be recommenced within the mere frame of unity attained. /

This candid attempt to take possession of the whole world must be made in the name and for the sake of science and creative activity. It is to release science and creative ability, and every stage in the struggle must be watched and criticised, lest there be any sacrifice of these ends to the exigencies of conflict.

The security of creative progress and creative activity implies a competent regulation of the economic life in the collective interest. There must be food, shelter and leisure for all. The fundamental needs of the animal life must be assured before human life can have free play. Man does not live by bread alone ; he eats that he may learn and adventure creatively, but unless he eats he cannot adventure. His life is primarily economic, as a house is primarily a foundation, and economic justice and efficiency must underlie all other activities, but to judge human society and organise political and social activities entirely on economic grounds is to forget the objectives of life's campaign in a preoccupation with supply.

It is true that man, like the animal world in general from which he has arisen, is the creature of a struggle for sustenance, but unlike the animals, man can resort to methods of escape from that competitive pressure upon the means of subsistence, which has been the lot of every other animal species. He can restrain the increase in his numbers and he seems capable of still quite undefined expansions of his productivity per head of population. He can escape therefore from the struggle for subsistence altogether with a surplus of energy such as no other kind of animal species has ever possessed. Intelligent control of population is a possibility which puts man outside the competitive processes that have hitherto ruled the modification of species, and he can be released from these processes in no other way.

There is a clear hope that later, directed breeding will come within his scope, but that goes beyond his present range of practical achievement, and we need not discuss it further here. Suffice it for us here that the world community of our desires, the organised world community conducting and ensuring its own progress, requires a deliberate collective control of population as a primary condition.

There is no strong instinctive desire for multitudinous offspring as such, in the feminine make-up. The reproductive impulses operate indirectly. Nature ensures a pressure of population through passions and instincts that, given sufficient knowledge, intelligence and freedom on the part of women, can be satisfactorily gratified and tranquillised if need be, without the production of numerous children. Very slight adjustments in social and economic arrangements will, in a world of clear available knowledge and straightforward practice in these matters, supply sufficient inducement or discouragement to affect the general birthrate or the birthrate of specific types as the directive sense of the community may consider desirable. So long as the majority of human beings are begotten involuntarily in lust and ignorance, so long does man remain like any other animal under the moulding pressure of competition for subsistence. Social and political processes change entirely in their character when we recognise the possibility and practicability of this fundamental revolution in human biology.

In a world so relieved, the production of staple necessities presents a series of problems altogether less distressful than those of the present scramble for possessions and self-indulgence on the part of the successful and for work and a bare living on the part of the masses. With the increase of population unrestrained there was, as the end of the economic process, no practical alternative to a multitudinous equality at the level of bare subsistence, except through such an inequality of economic arrangements as allowed a minority to maintain a higher standard of life by withholding whatever surplus of production it could grasp, from consumption in mere proletarian increase. In the past and at present, what is called the capitalist system, that is to say the unsystematic exploitation of production by private owners under the protection of the law, has, on the whole, in spite of much haste and conflict, worked beneficially, by checking the gravitation to a universal low-grade consumption which would have been the inevitable outcome of socialism oblivious of biological processes. With effective restraint upon the increase of population, however, entirely new possibilities open out before mankind.

The besetting vice of economic science, orthodox and unorthodox alike, has been the vice of beginning in the air, with current practice and current convictions, with questions of wages, prices, values and possession, when the profounder issues of human association are really not to be found at all on these levels. The primary issues of human association are biological and psychological, and the essentials of economics are problems in applied physics and chemistry. The first thing we should examine is what we want to do with natural resources, and the next, how to get men to do what has to be done as pleasurably and effectively as possible. Then we should have a standard by which to judge the methods of to-day.

But the academic economists and still more so Marx and his followers, refuse to deal with these fundamentals, and with a stupid air of sound practical wisdom, insist on opening up their case with an uncritical acceptance of the common antagonism of employers and employed and a long rigmarole about profits and wages. Ownership and expropriated labour are only one set of many possible sets of economic method.

The economists however will attend seriously only to the current set, the rest they ignore, and the Marxists with their uncontrollable disposition to use nicknames in the place of judgments, condemn all others as " Utopian "—a word as final in its dismissal from the minds of the elect as that other pet counter in the Communist substitute for thought, " Bourgeois." If they can persuade themselves that an idea or a statement is " Utopian " or " Bourgeois," it does not seem to matter in the least to them whether it is right or wrong. It is disposed of. Just as in genteeler circles anything is disposed of that can be labelled " atheistical," " subversive " or " disloyal."

If a century and a half ago the world had submitted its problems of transport to the economists they would have put aside, with as little wasted breath and ink as possible, all talk about railways, motor-cars, steamships and aeroplanes, and, with a fine sense of extravagance rebuked, set themselves to long neuralgic dissertations, disputations and treatises upon high-roads and the methods of connecting them, turnpike gates, canals, the influence of lock-fees on bargemen, tidal landing places, anchorages, surplus carrying capacity, carriers, caravans, hand-barrows and the pedestrianariat. There would have been a rapid and easy differentiation in feeling and requirements between the horse-owning minority and the walking majority ; the wrongs of the latter would have tortured the mind of every philosopher who could not ride and been minimised by every philosopher who could, and there would have been a broad rift between the narrow footpath school, the no footpath school and the school which would look forward to a time when every horse would have to be led along one universal footpath under the dictatorship of the pedestrianariat. All with the profoundest gravity and dignity. These things, footpaths and roads and canals with their traffic, were " real," and " Utopian " projects for getting along at thirty or forty miles an hour or more up hill and against wind and tide, let alone the still more incredible suggestion of air transport, would have been smiled and sneered out of court. Life went about on its legs, with a certain assistance from wheels, or floated, rowed and was blown about on water ; so it had been—and so it would always be.

But as soon as this time-honoured pre-occupation with the allotment of the shares of originators, organisers, workers, owners of material, credit dealers an l tax collectors in the total product, ceases to be dealt with as the primary question in economics, as soon as we liberate our minds from a pre-occupation which from the outset necessarily makes that science a squabble rather than a science, and begin our attack upon the subject with a survey of the machinery and other productive material required in order that the staple needs of mankind should be satisfied, if we go on from that to consider the way in which all this material and machinery can be worked and the product distributed with the least labour and the greatest possible satisfaction, we shift our treatment of economic questions towards standards by which all current methods of exploitation, employment and finance can be judged rather than wrangled over. We can dismiss the question of the claims of this sort of participant or that, for later and subordinate consideration, and view each variety of human assistance in the general effort entirely from the standpoint of what makes that assistance least onerous and most effective.

The germs of such really scientific economics exist already in the study of industrial organisation and industrial psychology. As the science of industrial psychology in particular develops, we shall find all this discussion of ownership, profit, wages, finance and accumulation, which has been treated hitherto as the primary issues of economics, falling into place under the larger enquiry of what conventions in these matters, what system of money and what conceptions of property, yield the greatest stimulus and the least friction in that world-wide system of co-operation which must constitute the general economic basis to the activities of a unified mankind.

Manifestly the supreme direction of the complex of human economic activities in such a world must centre upon a bureau of information and advice, which will take account of all the resources of the planet, estimate current needs, apportion productive activities and control distribution. The topographical and geological surveys of modern civilised communities, their government maps, their periodic issue of agricultural and industrial statistics, are the first crude and inco-ordinated beginnings of such an economic world-intelligence. In the propaganda work of David Lubin, a pioneer whom mankind must not forget, and in his International Institute of Agriculture in Rome, there were the beginnings of an impartial review month by month and year by year of world production, world needs and world transport. Such a great central organisation of economic science would necessarily produce direction ; it would indicate what had best be done here, there and everywhere, solve general tangles, examine, approve and initiate fresh methods and arrange the transitional process from old to new. It would not be an organisation of will, imposing its will upon a reluctant or recalcitrant race ; it would be a direction, just as a map is a direction. A map imposes no will on anyone, breaks no one in to its " policy." And yet we obey our maps.

The will to have the map, full, accurate and up-to-date and the determination to have its indications respected, would have to pervade the whole community. To nourish and sustain that will must be the task not of any particular social or economic division of the community but of the whole body of religious-minded people in that community. The organisation and preservation of that power of will is the primary undertaking, therefore, of a world revolution aiming at universal peace, welfare and happy activity.

The older and still prevalent conception of government is bullying, is the breaking-in and subjugation of the " subject," to the God, or King, or Lords of the community. Will-bending, the overcoming of the recalcitrant junior and inferior, was an essential process in the establishment of primitive societies, and its tradition still rules our education and law. No doubt there must be a necessary accommodation of the normal human will to every form of society ; no man is immaculately virtuous ; but compulsion and restraint are the friction of the social machine and, other things being equal, the less compulsive social arrangements are, the more willingly, naturally and easily they are accepted, the less wasteful of moral effort and the happier, that community will be. The ideal state, other things being equal, is the state with the fewest possible number of will fights and will suppressions. This must be a primary consideration in determining the economic, biological and mental organisation of the world community at which we aim.

We have advanced the opinion that the control of population pressure is practicable without any violent conflict with " human nature," that given a proper atmosphere of knowledge and intention, there need be far less suppression of will in relation to production than prevails to-day. In the same way, it is possible that the general economic life of mankind may be made universally satisfactory, that there may be an abundance out of all comparison greater than the existing supply of things necessary for human well-being, freedom and activity, with not merely not more, but infinitely less subjugation and enslavement than now occurs. Man is still but half born out of the blind struggle for existence and his nature still partakes of the infinite wastefulness of his mother Nature. He has still to learn how to price the commodities he covets in terms of human life. He is indeed only beginning to realise that as something to be learnt. He wastes will and human possibility extravagantly in his current economic methods.

We know nowadays that the nineteenth century expended a great wealth of intelligence upon a barren controversy between Individualism and Socialism. They were treated as mutually exclusive alternatives instead of being questions of degree. Human society has been, is and always must be an intricate system of adjustments between unconditional liberty and the disciplines and subordinations of co-operative enterprise. Affairs do not move simply from a more individualist to a more socialist state or vice versa ; there may be a release of individual initiative going on here and standardisation or restraint increasing there. Personal property never can be socially guaranteed and yet unlimited in action and extent as the extremer individualists desired, nor can it be " abolished " as the extremer socialists proposed. Property is not robbery, as Proudhon asserted ; it is the protection of things against promiscuous and mainly wasteful use. In some cases it may restrict or forbid a use of things that would be generally advantageous, and it may be and is frequently unfair in its assignment of initiative, but the remedy for that is not an abolition but a revision of property. In the concrete it is a form necessary for liberty of action upon material, while abstracted as money, that liquidated generalised form of property, it is a ticket for individual liberty of movement and individual choice of reward.

The economic history of mankind is a history of the operation of the idea of property ; it relates the conflict of the unlimited acquisitiveness of egoistic individuals against the resentment of the disinherited and unsuccessful and the far less effective consciousness of a general welfare. Money grew out of a system of abstracting conventions and has been subjected to a great variety of restrictions, monopolisations and regulations. It has never been an altogether logical device and it has permitted the most extensive and complex developments of credit, debt and dispossession. All these developments have brought with them characteristic forms of misuse and corruption. The story is intricate and the tangle of relationships of dependence, of pressure, of interception, of misdirected services, crippling embarrassments and crushing obligations in which we live to-day admits of no such simple and general solutions as many exponents of socialism, for example, seem to consider possible.

But the thought and investigations of the past century or so have made it clear that a classification of property according to the nature of the rights exercisable and according to the range of ownership involved must be the basis of any system of social justice in the future.

Certain things, the ocean, the air, rare wild animals, must be the collective property of all mankind and cannot be altogether safe until they are so regarded, and until some concrete body exists to exercise these proprietary rights. Whatever collective control exists must protect these universal properties, the sea from derelicts, the strange shy things of the wild from extermination by the hunter and the foolish collector. The extinction of many beautiful creatures is one of the penalties our world is paying for its sluggishness in developing a collective common rule. And there are many staple things and general needs that now also demand a unified control in the common interest. The raw material of the earth should be for all, not to be monopolised by any acquisitive individual or acquisitive sovereign state, and not to be withheld from exploitation for the general benefit by any chance claims to territorial priority of this or that backward or bargaining person or tribe.

In the past, most of these universal concerns have had to be left to the competitive enterprise of profit-seeking individuals because there were as yet no collectivities organised to the pitch of ability needed to develop and control these concerns, but surely nobody in his senses believes that the supply and distribution of staple commodities about the earth by irresponsible persons and companies working entirely for monetary gain, is the best possible method from the point of view of the race as a whole. The land of the earth, all utilisable natural products, have fallen very largely under the rules and usages of personal property because that was the only recognised and practicable form of administrative proprietorship in the past. The development both of extensive proprietary companies and of government departments with economic functions has been a matter of the last few centuries, the development that is to say of communal, more or less impersonal ownership, and it is only through these developments that the idea of organised collectivity of proprietorship has become credible.

Even in quite modern state enterprises there is a tendency to recall the rôle of the vigilant, jealous and primitive personal proprietor in the fiction of ownership by His Majesty the King. In Great Britain, for example, George Rex is still dimly supposed to hover over the Postmaster General of his Post Office, approve, disapprove and call him to account. But the Postal Union of the world which steers a registered letter from Chile to Norway or from Ireland to Pekin is almost completely divorced from the convention of an individual owner. It works ; it is criticised without awe or malice. Except for the stealing and steaming of letters by the political police of various countries, it works fairly well. And the only force behind it to keep it working well is the conscious common sense of mankind.

But when we have stipulated for the replacement of individual private ownership by more highly organised forms of collective ownership, subject to free criticism and responsible to the whole republic of mankind, in the general control of sea and land, in the getting, preparation and distribution of staple products and in transport, we have really named all the possible generalisations of concrete ownership that the most socialistic of contemporaries will be disposed to demand. And if we add to that the necessary maintenance of a money system by a central world authority upon a basis that will make money keep faith with the worker who earns it, and represent from first to last for him the value in staple commodities he was given to understand it was to have, and if we conceive credit adequately controlled in the general interest by a socialised world banking organisation, we shall have defined the entire realm from which individual property and unrestricted individual enterprise have been excluded. Beyond that, the science of social psychology will probably assure us that the best work will be done for the world by individuals free to exploit their abilities as they wish. If the individual landowner or mineral-owner disappears altogether from the world, he will probably be replaced over large areas by tenants with considerable security of tenure, by householders and by licensees under collective proprietors. It will be the practice, the recognised best course, to allow the cultivator to profit as fully as possible by his own individual productivity and to leave the householder to fashion his house and garden after his own desire.

Such in the very broadest terms is the character of the world commonweal towards which the modern imagination is moving, so far as its direction and economic life are concerned. The organisation of collective bodies capable of exercising these wider proprietorships which cannot be properly used in the common interest by uncorrelated individual owners, is the positive practical problem before the intelligent portion of mankind to-day. The nature of such collective bodies is still a series of open questions, even upon such points as whether they will be elected bodies or groups deriving their authority from other sanctions. Their scope and methods of operation, their relations to one another and to the central bureau of intelligence, remain also to be defined. But before we conclude this essay we may be able to find precisions for at least the beginning of such definition.

Nineteenth-century socialism in its various forms, including the indurated formulæ of communism, has been a series of projects for the establishment of such collective controls, for the most part very

Dc

sketchy projects from which the necessary factor of a sound psychological analysis was almost completely wanting. Primarily movements of protest and revolt against the blazing injustices arising out of the selfishly individualistic exploitation of the new and more productive technical and financial methods of the eighteenth and nineteenth centuries, they have been apt to go beyond the limits of reasonable socialisation in their demands and to minimise absurdly the difficulties and dangers of collective control. Indignation and impatience were their ruling moods and if they constructed little they exposed much. We are better able to measure the magnitude of the task before us because of the clearances and lessons achieved by these pioneer movements.

CHAPTER VII

NO STABLE UTOPIA IS CON-TEMPLATED

This unified world towards which the efforts of the religious minority would direct human activities cannot be pictured for the reader as any static and stereotyped spectacle of happiness. Indeed one may doubt if such a thing as happiness is possible without steadily changing conditions involving continually enlarging and exhilarating opportunities. Mankind released from the pressure of population, the waste of warfare and the private monopolisation of the sources of wealth, will face the universe with a great and increasing surplus of will and energy. Change and novelty will be the order of life ; each day will differ from its predecessor in its greater amplitude of interest. Life which was once routine, endurance and mischance, will become adventure and discovery. It will no longer be " the old, old story."

We have still barely emerged from among the animals in their struggle for existence. We live only in the early dawn of human self-consciousness and in the first awakening of the spirit of mastery. We believe that the persistent exploration of our outward and inward worlds by scientific and artistic endeavour will lead to developments of power and activity upon which at present we can set no limits nor give any certain form.

Our antagonists are confusion of mind, want of courage, want of curiosity and want of imagination, indolence and spendthrift egotism. These are the enemies against which the Open Conspiracy arrays itself; these are the jailers of human freedom and achievement.

CHAPTER VIII

THE OPEN CONSPIRACY MUST BE HETEROGENEOUS

This open and declared intention of establishing a world order out of the present patchwork of particularist governments, of effacing the militarist conceptions that have hitherto given governments their typical form, and of removing credit and the broad fundamental processes of economic life out of reach of private profit-seeking and individual monopolisation, which is the substance of this Open Conspiracy to which the modern religious mind must necessarily address its practical activities, cannot fail to arouse enormous opposition. It is not a creative effort in a clear field ; it is a creative effort that can hardly stir without attacking established things. It is the repudiation of drift, of " leaving things alone." It criticises everything in human life from top to bottom and finds everything not good enough. It strikes at the universal human desire to feel that things are " all right."

One might conclude, and it would be a hasty unsound conclusion, that the only people to whom we could look for sympathy and any passionate energy in forwarding the revolutionary change would be the unhappy, the discontented, the dispossessed and the defeated in life's struggle. This idea lies at the root of the class-war dogmas of the

Marxists, and it rests on an entirely crude conception of human nature. The successful minority is supposed to have no effective motive but a desire to retain and intensify its advantages. A quite imaginary solidarity to that end is attributed to it, a preposterous base class activity. On the other hand, the unsuccessful mass—" proletariat "—is supposed to be capable of a clear apprehension of its disadvantages, and the more it is impoverished and embittered, the nearer draws its uprising, its constructive " dictatorship " and the Millennium.

No doubt a considerable amount of truth is to be found distorted in this theory of the communist revolution. Human beings, like other animals, are disposed to remain where their circumstances are tolerable and to want change when they are uncomfortable, and so a great proportion of the people who are " well off " want little or no change in present conditions, particularly those who are too dull to be bored by an unprogressive life—and a great proportion of those who actually feel the inconveniences of straitened means and population pressure, do. But much vaster masses of the rank and file of humanity are accustomed to inferiority and dispossession, they do not feel these things to the extent even of desiring change, or given so much apprehension they still fear change more than they dislike their disadvantages. Moreover, those who are sufficiently distressed to realise that " something ought to be done about it " are much more disposed to childish and threatening demands upon heaven and the government for redress and vindictive and punitive action against the envied fortunate with whom they happen to be in immediate contact, than to any reaction towards such complex, tentative disciplined constructive work as alone can better the lot of mankind. In practice Marxism is found to work out in a ready resort to malignantly destructive activities and to be so uncreative as to be practically impotent in the face of material difficulties. In Russia where—in and about the urban centres at least—Marxism has been put to the test, the doctrine of the Workers' Republic remains as a unifying cant, a test of orthodoxy of as little practical significance there as the communism of Jesus and communion with Christ in Christendom, while beneath this creed a small oligarchy which has attained power by its profession does its obstinate best, much hampered by the suspicion and hostility of the Western financiers and politicians, to carry on a series of interesting and varyingly successful experiments in the socialisation of economic life. Each year shows more and more clearly that Marxism and Communism are divagations from the path of human progress and that the line of advance must follow a course more intricate and less flattering to the common impulses of our nature.

The one main strand of truth in the theory of social development woven by Marx and Engels is that successful, comfortable people are disposed to dislike, obstruct and even resist actively any substantial changes in the current patchwork of arrangements, however great the ultimate dangers of that patchwork may be or the privations and sufferings of other people involved in it. The one main strand of error in that theory is the facile assumption that the people at a disadvantage will be stirred to anything more than chaotic and destructive expressions of resentment. If now we reject the error and accept the truth, we lose the delusive comfort of belief in that magic giant, the Proletariat, who will dictate, arrange, restore and create, but we clear the way for the recognition of an élite of intelligent religious-minded people scattered through the whole community, and for a study of the method of making this creative element effective in human affairs against the massive oppositions of selfishness and unimaginative self-protective conservatism.

Now certain classes of people such as thugs and burglars seem to be harmful to society without a redeeming point about them, and others such as race-course bookmakers seem to provide the minimum of distraction and entertainment with a maximum of mischief. Wilful idlers are a mere burthen on the community. Other social classes again, professional soldiers for example, have a certain traditional honourableness which disguises the essentially parasitic relationship of their services to the developing modern community. Armies and armaments are cancers produced by the malignant development of the patriotic virus under modern conditions of exaggeration and mass suggestion. But since there are armies prepared to act coercively in the world to-day, it is necessary that the Open Conspiracy should contain within itself the competence to resist military coercion and combat and destroy armies that stand in the way of its emergence. Possibly the first two types here instanced may be condemned as classes and excluded as classes from any participation in the organised effort to recast the world, but quite obviously the soldier cannot. The world commonweal will need its own scientific methods of prevention so long as there are people running about the planet with flags and uniforms and weapons, offering violence to their fellow men and interfering with the free movements of commodities in the name of national sovereignty.

And when we come to the general functioning classes, landowners, industrial organisers, bankers and so forth, who control the present system such as it is, it should be still plainer that it is very largely from the ranks of these classes and from their stores of experience and traditions of method, that the directive forces of the new order must emerge. The Open Conspiracy can have nothing to do with the heresy that the path of human progress lies through an extensive class war.

Let us consider how it stands to such a complex of activities, usages, accumulations, advantages as constitutes the banking world. There are no doubt many bankers and many practices in banking which make for personal or group advantage to the general detriment. They forestall, monopolise, constrain and extort and so increase their riches. And another large part of that banking world follows routine and established usage ; it is carrying on and keeping things going, and it is neither inimical nor conducive to the development of a progressive world organisation of finance. But there remains a residuum of original and intelligent people in banking or associated with banking or mentally interested in banking, who do realise that banking plays a very important and interesting part in the world's affairs, who are curious about their own intricate function and disposed towards a scientific investigation of its origins, conditions and future possibilities. Such types move naturally towards the Open Conspiracy. Their enquiries carry them inevitably outside the bankers' habitual field to an examination of the nature, drift and destiny of the entire human economic process.

Now the theme of the preceding paragraph might be repeated with variations through a score of paragraphs in which appropriate modifications would adapt it to the industrial organiser, the merchant and organiser of transport, the advertiser, the retail distributor, the agriculturalist, the engineer, the builder, the economic chemist, and a number of other types functional to the contemporary community. In all we should distinguish a base and harmful section, a mediocre section following established usage and an active, progressive section to whom we turn naturally for developments leading towards the progressive world commonweal of our desires. And our analysis might penetrate further than separation into types of individuals. In nearly every individual instance we should find a mixed composition, a human being of fluctuating moods and confused purposes, sometimes base, sometimes drifting with the tide and sometimes alert and intellectually and morally quickened. The Open Conspiracy must be content to take a fraction of a man, as it appeals to fractions of many classes, if it cannot get him altogether.

This idea of drawing together a proportion of all or nearly all the functional classes in contemporary communities in order to weave the beginnings of a world community out of their selection, is a fairly obvious one—and yet it has still to win practical recognition. Man is a morbidly gregarious and partisan creature ; he is deep in his immediate struggles ; the industrialist is best equipped to criticise his fellow industrialist, but he finds the root of all evil in the banker ; the wages worker shifts the blame for all social wrongs on the " employing class." There is an element of exasperation in most economic and social reactions and there is hardly a reforming or revolutionary movement in history which is not essentially an indiscriminate attack of one functioning class or type upon another, on the assumption that the attacked class is entirely to blame for the clash and that the attacking class is self-sufficient in the commonweal and can dispense with its annoying collaborator. A considerable element of justice enters into most such recriminations. But the Open Conspiracy cannot avail itself of these class animosities for its driving force. It can have therefore no uniform method of approach. For each class it has a conception of modification and development, and each class it approaches therefore at a distinctive angle. Some classes no doubt it would supersede altogether ; others—the scientific investigator for example—it must regard as almost wholly good and seek only to expand and empower, but it can no more adopt the prejudices and extravagances of any particular class as its basis than it can adopt the claims of any existing state or empire.

When it is clearly understood that the binding links of the Open Conspiracy we have in mind are certain broad general ideas and that—except perhaps in the case of scientific workers—we have no current set of attitudes of mind and habits of activity which we can turn over directly and unmodified to the service of the conspiracy, we are in a position to realise that the movement we contemplate must from the outset be diversified in its traditions and elements and various in its methods. It must fight upon several fronts and with many sorts of equipment. It will have a common spirit but it is quite conceivable that between many of its contributory factors there may be very wide gaps in understanding and sympathy.

CHAPTER IX

FORCES AND RESISTANCES IN THE GREAT MODERN COMMUNITIES NOW PREVALENT, WHICH WILL BE ANTAGONISTIC TO THE OPEN CONSPIRACY

We have now stated broadly but plainly the idea of the world commonweal which is the objective of the Open Conspiracy, and we have made a preliminary examination of the composition of the movement, showing that it must be necessarily not a class development but a convergence of many different sorts of people upon this common idea. Its opening task must be the elaboration, exposition and propaganda of this common idea, and, arising out of this, the incomparably vaster task of its realisation.

These are tasks not to be done *in vacuo* ; they have to be done in a dense world of crowding, incessant, passionate, unco-ordinated activities, the world of market and newspaper, seed-time and harvest, births, deaths, jails, hospitals, riots, barracks and army manœuvres, false prophets and royal processions, games and shows, fire, storm, pestilence, earthquake, war. Every day and every hour things will be happening to help or thwart, stimulate or undermine, obstruct or defeat the creative effort to set up the world commonweal.

Before we go on to discuss the selection and organisation of these heterogeneous and mainly religious impulses upon which we rest our hopes of a greater life for mankind, before we plan how these impulses may be got together into a system of co-ordinated activities, it will be well to review the main antagonistic forces with which, from its very inception, the Open Conspiracy will be—is now—in conflict.

To begin with, we will consider these forces as they present themselves in the highly developed Western European States of to-day and in their American derivatives, derivatives which in spite of the fact that in most cases they have far outgrown their lands of origin, still owe a large part of their social habits and political conceptions to Europe. All these States touch upon the Atlantic or its contributory seas ; they have all grown to their present form since the discovery of America ; they have a common association rooting in the idea of Christendom and a generic resemblance of method. They present what is known in current parlance as the Capitalist system, but it will relieve us of a considerable load of disputatious matter if we call them here simply the " Atlantic " civilisations and communities.

The consideration of these Atlantic civilisations in relation to the coming world civilisation will suffice for the present chapter. Afterwards we will consider the modification of the forces antagonistic to the Open Conspiracy as they display themselves beyond the formal confines of these now dominant States in the world's affairs, in the social systems weakened and injured by their expansion and among such less highly organised communities as still survive from man's savage and barbaric past.

The Open Conspiracy is not necessarily antagonistic to any existing government. The Open Conspiracy is a creative organising movement and not an anarchistic one. It does not want to destroy existing controls and forms of human association, but either to supersede or amalgamate them into a common world directorate. If constitutions, parliaments and kings can be dealt with as provisional institutions, trustees for the coming of age of the world commonweal, and in so far as they are conducted in that spirit, the Open Conspiracy makes no attack upon them.

But most governments will not set about their business as in any way provisional, they and their supporters insist upon a reverence and obedience which repudiate any possibility of supersession. What should be an instrument becomes a divinity. In nearly every country of the world there is, in deference to the pretended necessities of a possible war, a vast degrading and dangerous cultivation of loyalty and mechanical subservience to flags, uniforms, presidents and kings. A president or king who does his appointed work well and righteously is entitled to as much subservience as a bricklayer who does his work well and righteously and to no more, but instead there is a sustained endeavour to give him the privileges of an idol above criticism or reproach, and the organised worship of flags has become—with changed conditions of intercourse and warfare—an entirely evil misdirection of the gregarious impulses of our race. Emotion and sentimentality are evoked in the cause of disciplines and co-operations that could quite easily be sustained and that are better sustained by rational conviction.

The Open Conspiracy is necessarily opposed to all such implacable loyalties and still more so to the aggressive assertion and propaganda of such loyalties. When these things take the form of suppressing reasonable criticism and forbidding even the suggestion of other forms of government they become plainly antagonists to any comprehensive project for human welfare. They become manifestly, from the wider point of view, seditious, and loyalty to " king and country " passes into plain treason to mankind. Almost everywhere at present, educational activities organise barriers in the path of progress and there are only the feeblest attempts at any counter-education that will break up these barriers. There is little or no effort to restrain the aggressive nationalist when he waves his flag against the welfare of our race or to protect the children of the world from the infection of his enthusiasms. And this last is as true now of the American system as it is of any European State.

In the great mass of the modern community there is little more than a favourable acquiescence in patriotic ideas and in the worship of patriotic symbols, and that is based largely on such training. These things are not necessary things for the generality to-day. A change of mental direction would be possible for the majority of people now without any violent disorganisation of their intimate lives or any serious social or economic readjustments for them. Mental infection in such cases could be countered by mental sanitation. A majority of people in Europe and a still larger majority in the United States and the other American Republics could become citizens of the world without any serious hindrance to their present occupations, and with incalculably vast increase of their present security.

But there remains a net of special classes in every community, from kings to custom-house officers, far more deeply involved in patriotism because it is their trade and their source of honour, and prepared in consequence with an instinctive resistance to any re-orientation of ideas towards a broader outlook. In the case of such people no mental sanitation is possible without dangerous and alarming changes in their way of living. For the majority of these patriots by *métier*, the Open Conspiracy unlocks the gates leading from a paradise of eminence, respect and privilege, and motions them towards an outer wilderness which does not present even the faintest promise of a congenial, distinguished life for them. Nearly everything in human nature will dispose them to turn away from these gates which open towards the world peace, to bang-to and lock them again if they can, and to grow thickets as speedily as possible to conceal them and get them forgotten. The suggestion of being trustees in a transition will seem to most of such people only the camouflage of an ultimate degradation.

From such classes of patriots by *métier*, it is manifest that the Open Conspiracy can expect only opposition. It may detach individuals from them, but only

Ec

by depriving them of their essential class loyalties and characteristics. The class as a class will remain none the less antagonistic. About royal courts and presidential residences, in diplomatic, consular, military and naval circles and wherever people wear titles and uniforms and enjoy pride and precedences based on existing political institutions, there will be the completest general inability to grasp the need for the Open Conspiracy. These people and their womankind, their friends and connections, their servants and dependants are fortified by time-honoured traditions of social usage, of sentiment and romantic prestige. They will insist that they are reality and Cosmopolis a dream. Only individuals of exceptional imaginative liveliness, rare intellectual power and innate moral force can be expected to break away from the anti-progressive habits such class conditions impose upon them.

This tangle of traditions and loyalties, of interested trades and professions, of privileged classes and official patriots, this complex of human beings embodying very easy and natural and time-honoured ideas of eternal national separation and unending international and class conflict, is the main objective of the Open Conspiracy in its opening phase. This tangle must be disentangled as the Open Conspiracy advances, and until it is largely disentangled and cleared up that Open Conspiracy cannot become anything very much more than a desire and a project.

The tangle of " necessary patriots " as one may call them is different in its nature, less intricate and extensive proportionally in the United States and the States of Latin America than it is in the old European communities, but it is none the less virulent in its action on that account. It is only recently that military and naval services have become important factors in American social life, and the really vitalising contact of the interested patriot and the State has hitherto centred mainly upon the custom-house and the concession. Instead of a mellow and romantic loyalty to "king and country" the American thinks simply of America and his flag.

American independence began as a resistance to exploitation from overseas. Even when political and fiscal freedom were won, there was a long phase of industrial and financial dependence. The American's habits of mind, in spite of his recent realisation of the enormous power and relative prosperity of the United States and of the expanding possibilities of their Spanish and Portuguese-speaking neighbours, are still largely self-protective against a now imaginary European peril. For the first three quarters of the nineteenth century the people of the American continent and particularly the people of the United States felt the industrial and financial ascendency of Great Britain and had a reasonable fear of European attacks upon their continent. A growing tide of immigrants of uncertain sympathy threatened their dearest habits. Flag worship was imposed primarily as a repudiation of Europe. Europe no longer looms over America with overpowering intimations, American industries no longer have any practical justification for protection, American finance would be happier without it, but the patriotic interests are so established now that they go on and will go on.

We have said that the complex of classes in any country interested in the current method of government is sustained by traditions and impelled by its nature and conditions to protect itself against exploratory criticism. It is therefore unable to escape from the forms of competitive and militant nationalism in which it was evolved. It cannot without grave danger of enfeeblement, change any such innate form. So that while parallel complexes of patriotic classes are found in greater or less intricacy grouped about the flags and governments of most existing states, these complexes are by their nature obliged to remain separate, nationalist and mutually antagonistic. You cannot expect a world union of soldiers or diplomatists. Their existence and nature depend upon the idea that national separation is real and incurable, and that war, in the long run, is unavoidable. Their conceptions of loyalty involve an antagonism to all foreigners, even to foreigners of exactly the same types as themselves, and make for a continual campaign of annoyances, suspicions and precautions—together with a general propaganda, affecting all other classes, of the necessity of an international antagonism—that creeps persistently towards war.

But while the methods of provoking war employed by the patriotic classes are traditional, modern science has made a new and enormously more powerful thing of warfare and, as the Great War showed, even the most conservative generals on both sides are unable to prevent the gigantic interventions of the mechanician and the chemist. So that a situation is brought about in which the militarist element is unable to fight without the support of the modern industrial organisation and the acquiescence of the great mass of people. We are confronted therefore at the present time with the paradoxical situation that a patriotic tradition sustains in power and authority warlike classes who are quite incapable of carrying on war. The other classes to which they must go for support when the disaster of war is actually achieved are classes developed under peace conditions, which not only have no positive advantage in war, but must, as a whole, suffer great dislocation, discomfort, destruction and distress from war. It is of primary importance to the formally dominant classes that these new social masses and powers should remain under the sway of the old social, sentimental and romantic traditions, and equally important is it to the Open Conspiracy that they should be released.

Here we bring into consideration another great complex of persons, interests, traditions—the world of education, the various religious organisations, and, beyond these, the ramifying indeterminate world of newspapers and other periodicals, books, the drama, art and all the instruments of presentation and suggestion that mould opinion and direct action. The sum of the operations of this complex will be either to sustain or demolish the old nationalist militant ascendency. Its easiest immediate course is to accept it. Educational organisations on that account are now largely a conservative force in the community ; they are in most cases directly controlled by authority and bound officially as well as practically to respect current fears and prejudices. It evokes fewer difficulties for them if they limit and mould rather than release the young. The school-master tends therefore to accept and standardise and stereotype, even in the living, progressive fields of science and philosophy. Even there he is a brake on the forward movement. It is clear that the Open Conspiracy must either continually disturb and revivify him or else frankly antagonise him. Universities also struggle between the honourable past on which their prestige rests, and the need of adaptation to a world of enquiry, experiment and change. It is an open question whether these particular organisations of intellectual prestige are of any real value in the living world. A modern world planned *de novo* would probably produce nothing like a contemporary University. Modern research, one may argue, would be stimulated rather than injured by complete detachment from the lingering mediævalism of such institutions, their entanglement with adolescent education and their ancient and contagious conceptions of precedence and honour.

Ordinary religious organisations, again, exist for self-preservation and are prone to follow rather than direct the currents of popular thought. They are kept alive indeed by revivalism and new departures which at the outset they are apt to resist, as the Catholic Church for instance resisted the Franciscan awakening, but their formal disposition is conserva-tive. They say to religious development, thus far and no farther.

Here in school, college and church are activities

of thought and instruction, which generally speaking drag upon the wheels of progress, but which need not necessarily do so. A schoolmaster may be original, stimulating and creative, and if he is fortunate and a good fighter he may even achieve considerable worldly success; University teachers and investigators may strike out upon new lines and yet escape destruction by the older dons. Universities compete against other Universities at home and abroad and cannot altogether yield to the forces of dullness and subservience. They must maintain a certain difference from vulgar opinion and a certain repute of intellectual virility.

As we pass from the more organised to the less organised intellectual activities, we find conservative influence declining in importance and a freer play for the creative drive. Freshness is a primary condition of journalistic, literary and artistic success, and orthodoxy has nothing new to say or do. But the desire for freshness may be satisfied all too readily by merely extravagant, superficial and incoherent inventions.

The influence of the old traditional nationalist social and political hierarchy is not, however, exerted exclusively through its control over schools and Universities. Nor is that indeed its more powerful activity. Would that it were ! There is also a direct, less defined contact of the old order with the nascent powers, that plays a far more effective part in delaying the development of the modern world commonweal. Necessarily the old order has determined the established way of life, which is at its best large, comfortable, amusing, respected. It possesses all the entrances and exits and all the controls of the established daily round. It is able to exact and it does exact, almost without design, many conformities. There can be no very ample social life therefore for those who are conspicuously dissentient. Again the old order has a complete provision for the growth, welfare and advancement of its children. It controls the founts of honour and self-respect ; it provides a mapped-out world of behaviour. The new initiatives make their appearance here and there in the form of isolated individuals, here an inventor, there a bold organiser or a vigorous thinker. Apart from his specific work the innovating type finds that he must fall in with established things or his womenfolk will be ostracised and he will be distressed by a sense of isolation even in the midst of successful activities. The more intensely he innovates in particular, the more likely is he to be too busy to seek out kindred souls and organise a new social life in general. The new things and ideas, even when they arise abundantly, arise scattered and unorganised, and the old order takes them in its net. America for example—both on its Latin and its English-speaking side—is in many ways a triumph of the old order over the new.

Men like Winwood Reade thought that the New World would be indeed a new world. They idealised its apparent emancipations. But as the more successful of the toiling farmers and traders of republican America rose one by one to affluence, leisure, and freedom, it was far more easy for them to adopt the polished and prepared social patterns and usages of Europe than to work out a complete new civilisation in accordance with their equalitarian professions. Yet there remains a gap in their adapted " Society." Henry James, that acute observer of subtle social flavours, has pointed out the peculiar *headlessness* of social life in America because of the absence of court functions to " go on " to and justify the assembling and dressing. The social life has imitated the preparation for the Court without any political justification. In Europe the assimilation of the wealthy European industrialist and financier by the old order has been parallel and naturally more logically complete. He really does find a court to " go on " to. His social scheme is still undecapitated.

In this way the complex of classes vitally involved in the old militant nationalist order is mightily reinforced by much larger masses of imitative and annexed and more or less assimilated rich and active people. The great industrialist marries the daughter of the marquis and has a couple of sons in the Guards and a daughter who is a princess. The money of the American Leeds, fleeing from the social futility of its land of origin, helps bolster up a mischievous monarchy in Greece. The functional and private life of the new men are thus at war with one another. The real interests of the great industrialist or financier lie in cosmopolitan organisation and the material development of the world commonweal, but his womenfolk pin flags all over him and his sons are prepared to sacrifice themselves and all his business creations, for the sake of trite splendours and Ruritanian romance.

But just so far as the great business organiser is capable and creative, so far is he likely to realise and resent the price in frustration that the old order obliges him to pay for amusement, social interest and domestic peace ánd comfort. The Open Conspiracy threatens him with no effacement ; it may even appear with an air of release. If he had women who were interested in his business affairs instead of women who had to be amused, and if he realised in time the practical, intellectual and moral kidnapping of his sons and daughters by the old order that goes on, he might pass quite easily from acquiescence to antagonism. But in this respect he cannot act single-handed. This is a social and not an individual operation. The Open Conspiracy, it is clear, must include in its activities a great fight for the souls of economically functional people. It must carve out a Society of its own from Society. Only by the creation of a new and better social life can it resist the many advantages and attractions of the old.

This constant gravitation back to traditional uses on the part of what might become new social types applies not merely to big people but to such small people as are really functional in the modern economic scheme. They have no social life adapted to their new economic relationships, and they are forced back upon the methods of behaviour established for what were roughly their 'analogues in the old order of things. The various sorts of managers and foremen in big modern concerns, for example, carry on ways of living they have taken ready made from the stewards, tradesmen, tenantry and upper servants of an aristocratic territorial system. They release themselves and are released almost in spite of themselves, slowly, generation by generation, from habits of social subservience that are no longer necessary nor convenient in the social process, acquire an official pride in themselves and take on new conceptions of responsible loyalty to a scheme. And they find themselves under suggestions of class aloofness and superiority to the general mass of less cardinal workers, that are often unjustifiable under new conditions. Machinery and scientific organisation have been and still are revolutionising productive activity by the progressive elimination of the unskilled worker, the hack, the mere toiler. But the social organisation of the modern community and the mutual deportment of the associated workers left over after this elimination are still haunted by the tradition of the lord, the middle class tenant and the servile hind. The development of self-respect and mutual respect among the mass of modern functional workers is clearly an intimate concern of the Open Conspiracy.

A vast amount of moral force has been wasted in the past hundred years by the antagonism of " Labour " to " Capital," as though this was the primary issue in human affairs. But this never was the primary issue and it is steadily receding from its former importance. The ancient civilisations did actually rest upon a broad basis of slavery and serfdom. Human muscle was a main source of energy—ranking with sun, rain and flood. But invention and discovery have so changed the conditions under which power is directed and utilised that muscle becomes economically secondary and inessential. We no longer want hewers of wood and drawers of water, carriers and pick and spade men. We no longer want that breeding swarm of hefty sweaty bodies without which the former civilisations could not have endured. We want watchful and understanding guardians and drivers of complex delicate machines, which can be mishandled and brutalised and spoilt all too easily. The less disposed these masters of our machines are to inordinate multiplication, the more room and food in the world for their ampler lives. Even to the lowest level of a fully mechanicalised civilisation it is required that the human element should be select. In the modern world, crowds are a survival and they will presently be an anachronism, and crowd psychology therefore cannot supply the basis of a new order.

It is just because labour is becoming more intelligent, responsible and individually efficient that it is becoming more audible and impatient in social affairs. It is just because it is no longer mere gang labour and becoming more and more intelligent co-operation in detail, that it now resents being treated as a serf, housed like a serf, fed like a serf and herded like a serf and its pride and thoughts and feelings disregarded. Labour is in revolt because as a matter of fact it is, in the ancient and exact sense of the word, ceasing to be labour at all.

The more progressive elements of the directive classes recognise this, but as we have shown, there are formidable forces still tending to maintain the old social attitudes when arrogance became the ruler and the common man accepted his servile status. A continual resistance is offered by large sections of the prosperous and advantaged to the larger claims of the modernised worker, and in response the rising and differentiating workers develop an angry antagonism to these directive classes which allow themselves to be controlled by their conservative and reactionary elements. Moreover, the increasing relative intelligence of the labour masses, the unprecedented imaginative stimulation they experience, the continually more widespread realisation of the available freedoms and comforts and indulgences that might be and are not shared by all in a modern state, develop a recalcitrance where once there was little but fatalistic acquiescence. An objection to direction and obligation, always mutely present in the toiling multitude since the economic life of man began, becomes articulate and active. It is the taste of freedom that makes labour desire to be free. This series of frictions is a quite inevitable aspect of social reorganisation but they do not constitute a primary antagonism in the process.

The class war was invented by the classes ; it is a natural tradition of the upper strata of the old order. It was so universally understood that there was no need to state it. It is implicit in nearly all the literature of the world before this nineteenth century— except the Bible, the Koran and other sequelæ. The " class war " of the Marxist is merely a poor snobbish imitation, a *tu quoque*, a pathetic, stupid, indignant reversal of and retort to the old arrogance, an *upward* arrogance.

These conflicts cut across rather than oppose or help the progressive development to which the Open

Conspiracy devotes itself. Labour, awakened, enquiring and indignant, is not necessarily progressive ; if the ordinary undistinguished worker is no longer to be driven as a beast of burthen, he has—which also goes against the grain—to be educated to as high a level of co-operative efficiency as possible. He has to work better, even if he works for much shorter hours and under better conditions, and his work must be subordinated work still ; he cannot become *en masse* sole owner and master of a scheme of things he did not make and is incapable of directing. Yet this is the ambition implicit in an exclusively " Labour " movement. Either the Labour revolutionary hopes to cadge the services of exceptional people without acknowledgment or return on sentimental grounds or he really believes that anyone is as capable as anyone else—if not more so. The worker at a low level may be flattered by dreams of " classconscious " mass dominion from which all sense of inferiority is banished, but they will remain dreams. The deep instinctive jealousy of the commonplace individual for outstanding quality and novel initiative may be organised and turned to sabotage and destruction, masquerading as and aspiring to be a new social order, but that will be a blind alley and not the road of progress. Our hope for the human future does not lie in crowd psychology and the indiscriminating rule of universal democracy.

The Open Conspiracy can have little use for mere resentments as a driving force towards its ends ; it starts with a proposal not to exalt the labour class but to abolish it, its sustaining purpose is to throw drudges out of employment and eliminate the inept—

and it is far more likely to incur suspicion and distrust in the lower ranks of the developing industrial order of to-day than to win support there. There, just as everywhere else in the changing social complexes of our time, it can appeal only to the exceptionally understanding individual who can without personal humiliation consider his present activities and relationships as provisional and who can, without taking offence, endure a searching criticism of his present quality and mode of living.

CHAPTER X

THE OPEN CONSPIRACY AND THE RESISTANCES OF THE LESS INDUSTRIALISED PEOPLES

So far in our accounting of the powers, institutions, dispositions, types and classes to which the Open Conspiracy will run counter, we have surveyed only such territory in the domain of the future world commonweal as is represented by the complex, progressive, highly industrialised communities, based on a preceding landlord-soldier, tenant, town-merchant and tradesman system, of the Atlantic type. These communities have developed farthest in the direction of mechanicalisation and they are so much more efficient and powerful that they now dominate the rest of the world. India, China, Russia, Africa present *mélanges* of social systems, thrown together, outpaced, overstrained, shattered, invaded, exploited and more or less subjugated by the finance, machinery and political aggressions of the Atlantic, Baltic and Mediterranean civilisation. In many ways they have an air of assimilating themselves to that civilisation, evolving modern types and classes and abandoning much of their distinctive traditions. But what they take from the West is mainly the new developments, the material achievements, rather than social and political achievements that, empowered by modern inventions, have won their way

to world predominance. They may imitate European
nationalism to a certain extent ; for them it becomes
a convenient form of self-assertion against the pressure of a realised practical, social and political inferiority ; but the degree to which they will or can
take over the social assumptions and habits of the
long-established European-American hierarchy is
probably very restricted. Their nationalism will remain largely indigenous ; the social traditions to
which they will try to make the new material forces
subservient will be traditions of an Oriental life
widely different from the original life of Europe.
They will have their own resistances to the Open
Conspiracy, therefore, but they will be different resistances from those we have hitherto considered. The
automobile and the wireless set, the harvester and
steel construction building, will come to the jungle
raja and the head hunter, the Brahmin and the
Indian peasant with a parallel and yet dissimilar
message to the one they brought the British landowner or the corn and cattle farmers of the Argentine
and the Middle West. Also they may be expected to
evoke dissimilar reactions.

To a number of the finer, more energetic minds of
these overshadowed communities which have lagged
more or less in the material advances to which this
present ascendency of Western Europe and America
is due, the Open Conspiracy may come with an
effect of immense invitation. At one step they may
go from the sinking vessel of their antiquated order,
across their present conquerors into a brotherhood
of world rulers. They may turn to the problem of
saving and adapting all that is rich and distinctive
Fc

of their inheritance to the common ends of the race. But to the less vigorous intelligences of this outer world, the new project of the Open Conspiracy will seem no better than a new form of Western envelopment, and they will fight a mighty liberation as though it were a further enslavement to the European tradition. They will watch the Open Conspiracy for any signs of conscious superiority and racial disregard. Necessarily they will recognise it as a product of Western mentality and they may well be tempted to regard it as an elaboration and organisation of current dispositions rather than the evolution of a new phase which will make no discrimination at last between the effete traditions of either East or West. Their suspicions will be sustained and developed by the clumsy and muddle-headed political and economic aggressions of the contemporary political and business systems, such as they are, of the West, now in progress. Behind that cloud of aggression Western thought has necessarily advanced upon them ; it could have got to their attention in no other way.

Partly these resistances and criticisms of the decadent communities outside the Atlantic capitalist systems will be aimed, not at the developing methods of the coming world community, but at the European traditions and restrictions that have imposed themselves upon these methods, and so far the clash of the East and West may be found to subserve the aims of the Open Conspiracy. In the conflict of old traditions and in the consequent deadlocks lies much hope for the direct acceptance of the groups of ideas centring upon the Open Conspiracy. One of the most interesting areas of humanity in this respect is the great system of communities under the sway or influence of Soviet Russia. Russia has never been completely incorporated with the European system ; she became a just passable imitation of a western European monarchy in the seventeenth and eighteenth centuries and talked at last of con-stitutions and parliaments—but the reality of that vast empire remained an Asiatic despotism and the European mask was altogether smashed by the successive revolutions of 1917. The ensuing system is a government presiding over an enormous extent of peasants and herdsmen, by a disciplined association professing the faith and dogmas of Marx, as inter-preted and qualified by Lenin.

In many ways this government is a novelty of extraordinary interest. In the fact that it is a pro-pagandist association becoming a commonweal, it is manifestly the inspiration and precursor of the Open Conspiracy. It labours against enormous difficulties within itself and without. Flung amazingly into a position of tremendous power, its intellectual flexibility is greatly restricted by the urgent militant necessity for mental unanimity and a consequent repression of criticism. It finds itself separated, intellectually and morally, by an enor-mous gap, from the illiterate millions over which it rules. More open perhaps to scientific and creative conceptions than any other government, and cer-tainly more willing to experiment and innovate, its enterprise is starved by the economic depletion of the country in the Great War and by the technical and industrial backwardness of the population upon which it must draw for its personnel. Moreover, it struggles within itself between concepts of a modern scientific social organisation and a vague anarchistic dream in which the " State " is to disappear and an emancipated proletariat, breeding and expectorating freely, fills the vistas of time for evermore. The tradition of heavy years of hopeless opposition have tainted the world policy of the Marxist cult with a mischievous and irritating quality that focuses upon it the animosity of every other government in the dominant Atlantic system. Nevertheless it has maintained itself for more than ten years and it seems far more likely to evolve than to perish. It is quite possible that it will evolve towards the conceptions of the Open Conspiracy, and in that case Russia may witness once again a conflict between new ideas and Old Believers. So far the Communist Party in Moscow has maintained a considerable propaganda of ideas in the rest of the world and especially across its western frontier. Many of these ideas are trite and stale. The time may be not far distant when the tide of propaganda will flow in the reverse direction. It has pleased the vanity of the Communist Party to imagine itself conducting a propaganda of world revolution. Its fate may be to develop upon lines that will make its more intelligent elements easily assimilable to the Open Conspiracy for a world revolution. The Open Conspiracy as it spreads and grows may find a less encumbered field for trying out the economic developments implicit in its conceptions in Russia and Siberia, than anywhere else in the world.

However severely the guiding themes and practical

methods of the present Soviet Government in Russia may be criticised, the fact remains that it has cleared out of its way many of the main obstructive elements that we find still vigorous in the more highly organised communities in the west. It has liberated vast areas from the kindred superstitions of monarchy and the need for a private proprietary control of great economic interests. And it has presented the Oriental China and India with the exciting spectacle of a social and political system capable of throwing off many of the most characteristic features of triumphant Westernism, and yet holding its own. In the days when Japan faced up to modern necessities, there were no models for imitation that were not communities of the Atlantic type pervaded by the methods of private capitalism, and in consequence the Japanese reconstituted their affairs on a distinctly European plan, adopting a Parliament and bringing their monarchy, social hierarchy and business and financial methods into a general conformity with that model. It is extremely doubtful whether any other Asiatic community will now set itself to a parallel imitation, and it will be thanks largely to the Russian revolution that this breakaway from Europeanisation has occurred.

But it does not follow that such a breakaway will necessarily lead more directly to the Open Conspiracy. If we have to face a less highly organised system of interests and prejudices in Russia and China, we have to deal with a vastly wider ignorance and a vastly more formidable animalism. Russia is a land of tens of millions of peasants ruled over by a little band of the intelligentsia who can be counted only by tens of thousands. It is only these few score thousands who are accessible to ideas of world construction, and the only hope of bringing the Russian system into active participation in the world conspiracy is through that small minority and through its educational repercussion on the myriads below. As we go eastward from European Russia the proportion of soundly prepared intelligence to which we can appeal for understanding and participation diminishes to an even more dismaying fraction. Eliminate that fraction and one is left face to face with inchoate barbarism incapable of social and political organisation above the level of the war boss and the brigand leader. Russia itself is still by no means secure against a degenerative process in that direction, and the hope of China struggling out of it without some forcible directive interventions is a hope to which constructive liberalism clings with very little assurance.

We turn back therefore from Russia, China and the communities of Central Asia to the Atlantic world. It is in that world alone that sufficient range and amplitude of thought and discussion is possible for the adequate development of the Open Con-spiracy. In these communities it must begin and for a long time its main activities will need to be sustained from these necessary centres of diffusion. It will develop amidst incessant mental strife and through that strife it will remain alive. It is no small part of the practical weakness of present day communism that it attempts to centre its intellectual life and its directive activities in Moscow and so cuts itself off from the free and open discussions of the Western world. Marxism lost the world when it went to Moscow and took over the traditions of Tzarism, as Christianity lost the world when it went to Rome and took over the traditions of Cæsar. Entrenched in Moscow from searching criticism, the Marxist ideology may become more and more dogmatic and unprogressive, repeating its sacred *credo* and issuing its disregarded orders to the proletariat of the world, and so stay ineffectively crystallised until the rising tide of the Open Conspiracy submerges, dissolves it afresh and incorporates whatever it finds assimilable.

India like Japan is cut off from the main body of Asiatic affairs. But while Japan has become a formally Westernised nationality in the comity of such nations, India remains a world in itself. In that one peninsula nearly every type of community is to be found, from the tribe of jungle savages through a great diversity of barbaric and mediæval principalities to the child and women sweating factories and the vigorous modern commercialism of Bombay. Over it all the British imperialism prevails, a constraining and restraining influence, keeping the peace, checking epidemics, increasing the food supply by irrigation and the like (so that population increases horribly), and making little or no effort to evoke responses to modern ideas. Britain in India is no propagandist of modern ferments : all those are left the other side of Suez. In India the Briton is a ruler as firm and self-assured and uncreative as the Roman. The old religious and social traditions, the complex customs, castes, tabus and exclusions of a strangely mixed but

unamalgamated community, though a little discredited by this foreign predominance, still hold
men's minds. They have been, so to speak, pickled in
the preservative of the British raj.

The Open Conspiracy has to invade the Indian
complex in conflict with the prejudices of both ruler
and governed. It has to hope for individual breaches
in the dull Romanism of the administration ; here a
genuine educationist, here a creative civil servant,
here an official touched by the distant stir of the
living homeland—and it has to try to bring these
types into a corporated relationship with a fine
native scholar here or an active-minded prince or
landowner or industrialist there. As the old methods
of passenger transport are superseded by flying, it
will be more and more difficult to keep the stir of the
living homeland out of either the consciousness of
the official hierarchy or the knowledge of the
recalcitrant " native."

Very similar to Indian conditions is the state of
affairs in the foreign possessions of France, the same
administrative obstacles to the Open Conspiracy
above, and below the same resentful subordination,
cut off from the mental invigoration of responsibility. Within these areas of restraint, India and its
lesser, simpler parallels in North Africa, Syria and
the Far East, there goes on a rapid increase cf low-
grade population, undersized physically and mentally, and retarding the mechanical development of
civilisation by its standing offer of cheap labour to
the unscrupulous entrepreneur, and possible feeble
insurrectionary material to the unscrupulous political
adventurer. It is impossible to estimate how slowly

or how rapidly the knowledge and ideas that have checked the rate of increase of all the Atlantic populations may be diffused through these less alert communities.

We must complete our survey of the resistances against which the Open Conspiracy has to work by a few words about the negro world and the regions of forest and jungle in which barbaric and even savage human life still escapes the infection of civilisation. It seems inevitable that the development of modern means of communication and the conquest of tropical diseases should end in giving access everywhere to modern administration and to economic methods, and everywhere the incorporation of the former wilderness in the modern economic process means the destruction of the material basis, the free hunting, the free access to the soil, of such barbaric and savage communities as still precariously survive. The dusky peoples, who were formerly the lords of these still imperfectly assimilated areas, are becoming exploited workers, slaves, serfs, hut-tax payers or labourers to a caste of white immigrants. The spirit of the plantation broods over all these lands. The negro in America differs only from his subjugated brother in South Africa or Kenya Colony in the fact that he also, like his white master, is an immigrant. The situation in Africa and America adjusts itself therefore towards parallel conditions, the chief variation being in the relative proportions of the two races and the details of the methods by which black labour is made to serve white ends.

In these black and white communities which are establishing themselves in all those parts of the earth where once the black was native, or in which a sub-tropical climate is favourable to his existence at a low level of social development, there is—and there is bound to be for many years to come—much racial tension. The steady advance of birth control may mitigate the biological factors of this tension later on, and a general amelioration of manners and conduct may efface that disposition to persecute dissimilar types, which man shares with many other gregarious animals. But meanwhile this tension increases and a vast multitude of lives is strained to tragic issues.

To exaggerate the dangers and evils of miscegenation is a weakness of our time. Man interbreeds with all his varieties and yet deludes himself that there are races of outstanding purity, the " Nordic," the " Semitic " and so forth. These are phantoms of the imagination. The reality is more intricate, less dramatic and grips less easily upon the mind ; the phantoms grip only too well and incite to terrible suppressions. Changes in the number of half-breeds and in the proportion of white and coloured are changes of a temporary nature that may become controllable and rectifiable in a few generations. But until this level of civilisation is reached, until the colour of a man's skin or the kinks in a woman's hair cease to have the value of Shibboleths that involve educational, professional and social extinction or survival, a black and white community is bound to be continually preoccupied by a standing feud too intimate and pervasive to permit of any long views of the world's destiny.

We come to the conclusion therefore that it is

from the more vigorous, varied and less severely obsessed centres of the Atlantic civilisations in the temperate zone, with their abundant facilities for publication and discussion, their traditions of mental liberty and their immense variety of interacting free modern types, that the main beginnings of the Open Conspiracy must develop. For the rest of the world, its propaganda, finding but poor nourishment in the local conditions, may retain a missionary quality for many years.

CHAPTER XI

RESISTANCES AND ANTAGONIS-TIC FORCES IN OURSELVES

We have dealt in the preceding two chapters with great classes and assemblages of human beings as, in the mass, likely to be more or less antagonistic to the Open Conspiracy, and it has been difficult in those chapters to avoid the implication that " we," some sort of circle round the writer, were aloof from these obstructive and hostile multitudes, and ourselves entirely identified with the Open Conspiracy. But neither are these multitudes so definitely against, nor those who are with us so entirely for, the Open Conspiracy to establish a world community as the writer in his desire for clearness and contrast and with an all too human disposition perhaps towards plain ego-centred combative issues, has been led to represent. There is no " we " and there can be no " we " in possession of the Open Conspiracy.

The Open Conspiracy is in partial possession of us and we attempt to serve it. But the Open Conspiracy is a natural and necessary development of contemporary thought arising here and there and everywhere. There are doubts and sympathies that weigh on the side of the Open Conspiracy in nearly everyone, and not one of us but retains many impulses, habits and ideas in conflict with our general devotion, checking and limiting our service.

Let us therefore in this chapter cease to discuss classes and types and consider general mental tendencies and reactions which move through all humanity.

In our opening chapters we pointed out that religion is not universally distributed throughout human society. And of no one does it seem to have complete possession. It seizes upon some of us and exalts us for one hour now and then, for a day now and then ; it may leave its afterglow upon our conduct for some time ; it may establish restraints and habitual dispositions ; sometimes it dominates us with but brief intermissions through long spells and then we can be saints and martyrs. In all our religious phases there appears a desire to *hold* the phase, to subdue the rest of our life to the standards and exigencies of that phase. Our quickened intelligence sets itself to a general analysis of our conduct and to the problem of establishing controls over our unilluminated intervals.

And when the religious elements in the mind set themselves to such self-analysis and attempt to order and unify the whole being upon this basis of the service and advancement of the race, they discover first a great series of indifferent moods, wherein the resistance to thought and work for the Open Conspiracy is merely passive and in the nature of inertia. There is a whole class of states of mind which may be brought together under the head of " everydayism." The dinner-bell and the playing-fields, the cinema and the newspaper, the week-end visit and the factory siren, a host of such expectant universal things, call to a vast majority of people in our modern world to stop thinking and get busy with the interest in hand, and so on to the next, without a thought for the general frame and drama in which these momentary and personal incidents are set. We are driven along these marked and established routes and turned this way or that by the accidents of upbringing, of rivalries and loves, of chance encounters and vivid experiences, and it is rare for many of us, and never for some, that the phases of broad reflection and self-questioning arise. For many people the religious life now, as in the past, has been a quite desperate effort to withdraw sufficient attention and energy from the flood of events to get some sort of grasp, and keep whatever grip is won, upon the relations of the self to the whole. Far more recoil in terror from such a possibility and would struggle strenuously against solitude in the desert, solitude under the stars, solitude in a silent room or indeed any occasion for comprehensive thought.

But the instinct and purpose of the religious type is to keep hold upon the comprehensive drama, and at the heart of all the great religions of the world we find a parallel disposition to escape in some manner from the aimless drive and compulsion of accident and everyday. Escape is attempted either by withdrawal from the presence of crowding circumstance into a mystical contemplation and austere retirement, or—what is more difficult and desperate and reasonable—by imposing the mighty standards of enduring issues upon the whole mass of transitory problems which constitute the actual business of life. We have already noted how the modern mind turns from retreat as a recognisable method of religion, and faces squarely up to the second alternative. The tumult of life has to be met and conquered. Aim must prevail over the aimless. Remaining in normal life we must yet keep our wills and thoughts aloof from normal life and fixed upon creative processes. However busied we may be, however challenged, we must yet save something of our best mental activity for self-examination and keep ourselves alert against the endless treacheries within that would trip us back into everydayism and disconnected responses to the stimuli of life.

Religions in the past, though they have been apt to give a preference to the renunciation of things mundane, have sought by a considerable variety of expedients to preserve the faith of those whom chance or duty still kept in normal contact with the world. Modern religion, which has no alternative to constant normal contact with the world, cannot lightly forgo the experiments of the old religions in such expedients. Meetings for mutual reassurance, confession and prayer, self-dedication, sacraments and seasons of fast and meditation need to be modernised or replaced by modern equivalents if the religious vitality of the Open Conspiracy is to be sustained. At present, except in the case of a few friends and lovers, the modern religious individual leads a life of extreme, wasteful and dangerous spiritual isolation. He may forget and he has nothing to remind him ; he may relapse and he will hear no reproach to warn him of his relapse.

"Everyday" has many ways of justifying the return

of the believer to its sceptical casualness. It is easy to
persuade oneself that one is taking life or oneself
" too seriously." The mind is very self-protective ; it
has a disposition to abandon too great or too far-
reaching an effort and return to things indisputably
within its scope. We have an instinctive preference for
thinking things are " all right " ; we economise
anxiety ; we defend the delusions that we can work
with, even though we half realise they are no more
than delusions. We resent the warning voice, the
critical question that robs our activities of assurance.
Our everyday moods are not only the antagonists of
our religious moods, but they resent all outward
appeals to our religious moods and they welcome
every help against religious appeals. We pass very
readily from the merely defensive to the defensive-
aggressive, and from refusing to hear the word that
might stir our consciences to a vigorous effort to
suppress its utterance.

Churches, religious organisations, try to keep the
revivifying phase and usage, where it may strike
upon the waning or slumbering faith of the convert,
but modern religion as yet has no such organised
reminders. They cannot be improvised. Crude
attempts to supply the needed corrective of conduct
may do less good than harm. Each one of us for
himself must do what he can to keep his high resolve
in mind and protect himself from the snare of his
own moods of fatigue or inadvertency.

But these passive and active defences of current
things which operate in and through ourselves, and
find such ready sympathy and assistance in the world
about us, these massive resistance systems, are only

the beginning of our tale of the forces antagonistic to the Open Conspiracy that lurk in our complexities.

Men are creatures with other faults quite beyond and outside our common disposition to be stupid, indolent, habitual and defensive. Not only have we active creative impulses but also acute destructive ones. Man is a jealous animal. In our youth and adolescence our egotism is extravagant. A great number of us at that stage would rather not see a beautiful or wonderful thing come into existence than have it come into existence disregarding us. Something of that jealous malice, self-assertive ruthlessness, there is in all of us. At his worst man can be an exceedingly combative, malignant, mischievous and cruel animal. And few of us —none of us—are altogether above the possibility of such phases. When we consider the oppositions to the Open Conspiracy that operate in the normal personality, we appreciate the soundness of the catechism which instructs us to renounce not only the trivial world and the heavy flesh, but the active and militant devil.

To make is a long and wearisome business, with many arrests and disappointments, but to break gives an instant thrill. We all know something of the delight of the *bang*. It is well for the Open Conspirator to ask himself at times how far he is in love with the dream of a world in order, and how far he is driven by hatred of institutions that bore or humiliate him. He may be no more than a revengeful incendiary in the mask of a constructive worker. How safe is he then from the reaction to some fresh

Gc

humiliation ? The Open Conspiracy which is now
his refuge and vindication may presently fail to give
him the compensation he has sought, may offer him
no better than a minor rôle, may display irritating
and incomprehensible preferences. And for a great
number of things in overt antagonism to the great
aim of the Open Conspiracy, he will still find within
himself not simply acquiescence but sympathy and
a genuine if inconsistent admiration. There they
are, waiting for his phase of disappointment. Back
he may go to the old loves with a new animus against
the greater scheme.

Man has pranced a soldier in reality and fancy for
so many generations that few of us can altogether
release ourselves from the brilliant pretensions of
flags, empire, patriotism and aggression. Business
men, especially in America, seem to feel a sort of
glory in calling even the underselling and over-
advertising of rival enterprises " fighting." Pill
vendors and public departments can have their
" wars," their heroisms, their desperate mischiefs,
and so get the Napoleonic feeling. The world and our
imaginations are full of the sentimentalities, the
false glories and loyalties of such refurbishing of the
old combative traditions, trailing after them, as
they do, so much worth and virtue in a dulled and
stupefied condition. It is difficult to resist the fine
·gravity, the high self-respect, examples of honour
and good style in small things, of the military and
naval services, for all that they are now no more than
noxious parasites upon the nascent world commonweal. In France not a word may be said against the
army ; in England, against the navy. There will be

many Open Conspirators at first who will scarcely dare to say that word even to themselves.

But all these obsolete values and attitudes with which our minds are cumbered must be cleared out if the new faith is to have free play. We have to clear them out not only from our own minds but from the minds of others who may be or become our associates. The finer and more picturesque false loyalties, false standards of honour, false religious associations, may seem to us, the more thoroughly must we seek to release our minds and the minds of those about us from them and cut off all thoughts of a return.

We cannot compromise with these vestiges of the ancient order. Whatever we retain of them will come back to life and grow again. It is no good to operate for cancer unless the whole growth is removed. Leave a crown about and presently you will find it being worn by someone resolved to be a king. Keep the name and image of a god without a distinct museum label and sooner or later you will discover a worshipper on his knees to it and be lucky not to find a human sacrifice upon the altar. Wave a flag and it will wrap about you. Of yourself even more than of the community is this true ; there can be no half measures. You have not yet completed your escape to the Open Conspiracy from the cities of the plain while it is still possible for you to take a single backward glance.

And at last when we conceive that we have given ourselves altogether to the Open Conspiracy frustra- tion may overtake us. Then it is, when we are assured that we are possessed by the Open Con- spiracy, that we shall be most disposed to think and act as though we possessed the Open Conspiracy. And if we have made sacrifices, if we are conscious of substantial success, then still more shall we be in danger. One of the most disagreeable features of Christian hagiology is the value set by the blessed saints upon their special privileges. The poor souls loved to think they had caught the peculiar attention of God by their sores and mortifications. This " weakness of the eminent claim " pervades all religions. Most of those who will serve the Open Conspiracy will be tempted to think they have deserved well and to compare their merits and their share of influence and recognition in the movement with those of others.

The Open Conspiracy will be no more free from rivalries, heartburnings, distrust, touchy suspicions, mutual interference and disingenuous negligences, than any other great human co-operation. The disciplines, the trainings and methods of organisation that must be evolved as the movement grows may be effective in restricting the mischief of such humanities ; they will certainly not suppress them altogether. Many a good and serviceable man may die embittered by the preoccupation of his fellow workers in this huge compaign. But the Open Conspiracy will grow as science grows, greater at last than all its outer antagonisms, than ancient tradition or instinctive resistance, greater than the conscious or unconscious disloyalties of its adherents, greater than all the present vices of mankind.

Beware of malice in this movement. Remember that man is a malicious animal and you are human.

Do not fall foul of your allies and associates because some of them affect your richer nature as prigs or pedants ; do not be too scrupulous about the motives of others ; your own also may be misconceived ; do not interpret enthusiastic service either as conceited self-assertion or calculated self-advancement, nor give way to excessive chagrin when some honourable task you had promised yourself is seized upon by someone else. Avoid the belittlement of useful work upon our side because it is not perfect. Do not let differences of accent and idiom annoy you. Many great movements have been crippled, many great opportunities lost, by the minor spites of the elect. Vindictive self-assertion is an invariable characteristic of the hopelessly damned. Watch yourself for the minutest first specks of this leprosy.

The Open Conspiracy may learn a useful lesson if it bears in mind the early phases of Christianity and Islam and guards itself against such sordid dissensions as sprung and enfeebled those mighty initiatives before even the first generation of disciples had passed away.

CHAPTER XII

THE OPEN CONSPIRACY MUST BEGIN AS A MOVEMENT OF EXPLANATION AND PROPAGANDA

And now, having taken the measure of the array of current things against which the Open Conspiracy must pit itself, we may go on to consider the germination and development of the Open Conspiracy.

It is fairly obvious that the primary and earliest task is to express, develop and propagate the idea of the Open Conspiracy, to make its external form clear, convincing, attractive and commanding to as many people as possible. The primary organisation must be a propagandist organisation.

The idea of the Open Conspiracy rests upon and arises out of a system of historical, biological and sociological realisations. In the case of people with sound knowledge in these fields we may look for these realisations already ; such people are prepared for adhesion without any great explanatory work ; there is nothing to set out to them but the project. They do already constitute the Open Conspiracy in an unorganised solution and will not so much adhere as admit to themselves and others their state of mind. Directly we pass beyond that comparatively restricted world, however, we shall find that we have to deal with partial knowledge, distorted views or blank ignorance, and that a revision and extension of historical and biological ideas and a considerable elucidation of economic misconceptions has to be undertaken.

For the past twelve years, the present writer has given much thought and work to the question of presenting these foundation ideas for a modern moral and political activity in a practicable form, and it will be the easiest method of statement for him to describe the outcome of his experiments and reflections. He reports therefore upon what he has done and is doing not because that is in any way final or universally applicable, but because it gives something sufficiently full and lucid to serve as a concrete illustration of his idea. He has schemed out a group of writings to embody the necessary ideas of the new time in a form adapted to the current reading public and he considers what he is doing as a sort of provisional " Bible," so to speak, for some factors at least in the Open Conspiracy. As the current reading public changes, his work will become obsolescent so far as its present form and method go. But not so far as its substantial method goes. That he believes will remain.

These writings, this modern Bible scheme, has taken a threefold form and he believes the mental basis of the Open Conspiracy must necessarily retain this threefold form if only on account of its lucidity of presentation. He has already written and published the opening third of his scheme, first in a full and then in a compacter book, as *The Outline of History* and as *A Short History of the World*. This furnishes a framework of fact within which the general political ideas of the reader can be put in order. It presents the history of life as a progress from fragmentation towards world unity, mental and material. A second third of this statement of fundamental modern ideas he is now preparing in collaboration with two more specially qualified writers. This will be a companion and parallel to the *Outline of History* and it will be called *The Science of Life*. It will be a summary of what is known of the nature and possibilities of life. It will give the data for personal conduct within a biologically conceived world society, just as the *Outline of History* gives a frame for the individual political life in a unifying world state. The remaining third of this encyclopædia, the third dealing mainly with inorganic and economic science, is still a mere sketch and skeleton. It will treat of economic and social organisation considered as the problem of man's exploitation of extraneous energy for the service of the species. Its prospective title, *The Conquest of Power*, will perhaps convey the spirit of its design. The general idea of these writings is to present altogether, first a complete modern world outlook, politically speaking, then the moral data of the new time, and then the forecast of a collective economic policy, in a form accessible to a person of ordinary education. It is the presentation of the threefold basis for a modern ideology, historical, biological and economic. It is a pioneer attempt to get this written down connectedly.

For a considerable section of the moderately educated public, with historical ideas fragmentary and restricted to mere periods and countries, the compilation of the *Outline of History* has served already, and still serves, as a stimulant and a release—and no doubt, when its work is supplemented by its two companions and when all that can be done now with life and matter is realised the three will help in a great number of cases to pull people's minds together into a shape that will dispose them to full participation in the new movement. But at the most exaggerated estimate possible, these works constitute a merely provisional " Bible," and the measure of their success will be marked by the promptitude of their replacement by worthier successors.

Such compilations cannot but have many of the characteristic defects of pioneer and elementary work ; they have often to achieve their ends by going rather roughly over secondary difficulties that would otherwise delay their production indefinitely. Yet at the outset they will be of use in marking out the shape and scope of the general concepts of the Open Conspiracy. At the outset, the Open Conspiracy, as it reaches beyond the range of exceptionally well-informed and mentally active people, must be very largely an educational propaganda of such material. Only later can it hope to relinquish this part of its task to renascent educational organisations which can be trusted to ensure a firm foundation for the modern conception of life.

The form in which the Open Conspiracy will first appear will certainly not be that of a centralised organisation. Its most natural and convenient method of coming into being will be the formation of small groups of friends, family groups, groups of

students and employees or other sorts of people
meeting and conversing frequently in the course of
their normal occupations, who will exchange views
and find themselves in agreement upon the general
idea. Fundamentally important issues upon which
unanimity must be achieved from the outset are,
firstly, the entirely provisional nature of all existing
governments, and the entirely provisional nature,
therefore, of all loyalties associated therewith ;
secondly, the supreme importance of population
control in human biology and the possibility it
affords us of a release from the pressure of the
struggle for existence on ourselves ; and thirdly, the
urgent necessity of protective resistance against the
present traditional drift towards war. People who
do not grasp the vital significance of these test issues
do not really begin to understand the Open Conspiracy. Groups coming into agreement upon these
matters, and upon their general interpretation of
history, will be in a position to seek adherents,
enlarge themselves and attempt to establish communication with kindred groups for common ends.
They can take up a variety of activities to develop
a sense and habit of combined action and feel their
way to greater enterprises.

We have shown already that the Open Conspiracy
must be heterogeneous in origin. Young men and
young women may be collected into groups arranged
upon lines not unlike those of the Bohemian Sokols
or the Italian Fasci. Such groups may easily have an
athletic and recreational side. These initial groups
will be of no uniform pattern. They will be of very
different size, average age, social experience and

influence. Their particular activities will be determined by these things. It is highly improbable that the name of the Open Conspiracy will be applied to any of them. That is just a provisional name in these Blue Prints. Their diverse qualities and influences will express themselves by diverse titles. A group of students may find itself capable of little more than self-education and personal propaganda ; a group of middle-class people in a small town may find its small resources fully engaged at first in such things as, for example, seeing that desirable literature is available for sale or in the local public library, protecting books and news-vendors from suppression, or influencing local teachers. Most parents of school-children can press for the teaching of universal history and sound biology and protest against the inculcation of aggressive patriotism. On the other hand, a group of ampler experience and resources may undertake the printing, publication and distribution of literature, and exercise considerable influence upon public opinion in turning education in the right direction. The League of Nations movement, the Birth Control movement and most radical and socialist societies are fields into which groups may go to find adherents more than half prepared for them. The Open Conspiracy is a fuller and ampler movement into which these incomplete activities must necessarily merge as its idea takes possession of men's imaginations.

From the outset, the Open Conspiracy will set its face against militarism. There is a plain present need for the organisation now, before war comes again, of an open and explicit refusal to serve in any war—or at most to serve in war, directly or indirectly, only after the issue has been fully and fairly submitted to arbitration. The time for a conscientious objection to war service is manifestly before and not after the onset of war. People who have acquiesced in a belligerent foreign policy by silence right up to the onset of war, have little to complain of if they are then compelled to serve. And a refusal to participate with one's country in warfare is a preposterously incomplete gesture unless it is rounded off by the deliberate advocacy of a world *pax*, a world economic control and a restrained population, such as the idea of the Open Conspiracy embodies.

The putting upon record of its members' reservation of themselves from any or all of the military obligations that may be thrust upon the country by military and diplomatic effort, will be, I think, the first considerable overt act of the Open Conspiracy groups. It will supply the practical incentive to bring many of them together in the first place. It will follow closely upon the beginning of the propaganda and it will probably necessitate the creation of regional or national *ad hoc* committees for the establishment of a collective legal and political defensive for this dissent from current militant nationalism. It will bring the Open Conspiracy very early out of the province of discussion into the field of practical conflict. It will from the outset invest it with a very necessary quality of present applicability.

The anticipatory repudiation of military service, so far as this last may be imposed by existing governments in their factitious international rivalries, need not necessarily involve a denial of the need of military action on behalf of the world commonweal for the suppression of nationalist brigandage, nor need it prevent the military training of members of the Open Conspiracy. It is simply the practical form of assertion that the normal militant diplomacy and warfare of the present time are offences against civilisation, processes in the nature of brigandage, sedition and civil war, and that serious men cannot be expected to play anything but a rôle of disapproval, non-participation or active prevention towards them. Our loyalty to our current government, we would intimate, is subject to its sane. and adult behaviour.

These educational and propagandist groups drawing together into an organised resistance to militarism and to the excessive control of individuals by the makeshift governments of to-day, are the possible and probable form in which the Open Conspiracy will appear in the world. But they constitute only the earliest and more elementary grade of its activities, and we will presently go on to consider the more specialised and constructive forms its effort must evoke. Before doing so, however, we may say a little more about the structure and method of these initiatory groups.

Since they are bound to be different and miscellaneous in form, size, quality and ability, any early attempts to organise them into common general action or even into regular common gatherings are to be deprecated. There should be many types of groups. Collective action had better for a time—perhaps for a long time—be undertaken not through the merging of groups but through the formation of *ad hoc* associations for definitely specialised ends. The groups will come into these associations to make a contribution very much as people come into limited liability companies, that is to say with a subscription and not with their whole capital. A comprehensive organisation attempting from the first to cover all activities would necessarily rest upon and promote one prevalent pattern of group and hamper or estrange the more original and interesting forms.

There is a detestable sort of energetic human being which preys upon human societies, delighting in procedure, by-laws, votings, stereotyping and embarrassing " resolutions," the " capture " of committees and organisations, the delegation of powers and suchlike politicians' mischief. It is a blighting and accursed type, living and multiplying in rules and precedents as bugs in old wallpaper. The less the Open Conspiracy devotes itself to such elaborations in its gatherings, the better for its spirit. Always it will be well to keep its comprehensive organisation easy and simple.

Each group should come together and develop its ideas, frankly and freely, at something like a common level of understanding and in a friendly atmosphere. It would be advisable that most groups should assemble with some regularity, and since in a large part of the world Sunday is recognised as the day set apart from the concerns of the individual for the consideration of wider issues, that day may well be the usual day for group gatherings. A weekly meeting at which everyone attempts to be present seems to be indicated as the normal habit of a group. A member who finds weekly attendance at his group meeting irksome, probably belongs to the wrong group and should seek another.

A normal group in the early stage of its existence will find most of its energy engaged in confirming and cleaning up its conception of the Open Conspiracy and in dealing with people invited to join in, trying out its ideas upon interested visitors and so forth. It will also experiment in outside activities determined by its special circumstances. The ordinary group must bear in mind that these practical activities must at first be preparatory and mainly self-educational. It must not subordinate its general mental task in them.

The clear conception of the Open Conspiracy is a considerable but necessary intellectual effort A group of historical, biological and economic ideas and interpretations has to be assimilated and they are not by any means simple and obvious ideas. And in addition—and what is perhaps the more difficult part—many prevalent habits of mind and current assumptions have to be got rid of. The conception of the Open Conspiracy involves, for example, a sceptical and destructive criticism of personal-immortality religions and also of the sacred formulæ of communism. It can work, and may go far in certain ways, with Christians or Communists, but it cannot incorporate them so long as they are Christians or Communists. Vague goodwill for mankind, or for progress, and adhesions based on some partial approval of its spirit, its methods or its objective, are of no real value to an enterprise so huge in its ultimate intentions.

For the furtherance of its aims, the Open Conspiracy may work in alliance with all sorts of movements and people, but to take them into its own essential substance is an altogether different matter. Propaganda and education are seed-sowing and only in revivalist religion is an immediate, a simultaneous reaping attempted with the sowing of the seed. The general run of people are more eager to do than to understand, and from the beginning of its first overt activities the Open Conspiracy will have to deal with the friendly advances of those who will want to share in its effort without any proper assimilation of the ideas that promote it. This will be another reason for projecting its practical activities into the form of *ad hoc* associations, into which outsiders with different or undeveloped religious, political, social and philosophical views may come without penetrating as permanent members into the actual groups, and it will also justify the helpful participation of the Open Conspiracy groups in definitely restricted movements which attend only to a portion of its programme. But many of those who first come into touch with the Open Conspiracy simply as helpers and allies will no doubt go on to a careful study of its general concepts and so to complete participation.

The groups of the Open Conspiracy, it may be reiterated, will vary much in leisure, knowledge, ability and scope. In the student world, in the associated world of special social, political and philosophical studies and in the world where speculative thought is combined with writing and discussion, groups will appear which turn naturally to the development and expression of the Open Conspiracy as their distinctive contribution. The concepts of the Open Conspiracy will appear increasingly in books and periodicals until some of these latter become recognised definitely as means of communication within the movement. It will acquire or provoke its own periodic literature. Such circles of " intelligentsia " will also supply lecturers and leaders of discussions who will be drawn upon by other groups and group combinations for visits of stimulus and elucidation.

From that, the spreading, growing and ripening groups will go on to combine with one another for local and regional meetings. People who have met first in *ad hoc* activities will find themselves developing naturally and progressively into social association and a loose general organisation with the Open Conspiracy. Such an organisation should leave the fullest scope for group or even individual autonomy in particular cases. The only binding restraint upon independent initiatives in the Open Conspiracy should be its broad essential requirements, namely :

(1) The complete assertion, practical as well as theoretical, of the provisional nature of existing governments and of our acquiescence in them ;

(2) The resolve to minimise by all available means the conflicts of these governments, their militant use of individuals and property and their interferences with the establishment of a world economic system ;

(3) The determination to replace private local or national ownership of at least credit, transport and staple production by a responsible world directorate serving the common ends of the race ;

Hc

(4) The practical recognition of the necessity for world biological controls, for example, of population and disease ;

(5) The support of a minimum standard of individual freedom and welfare in the world ; and

(6) The supreme duty of subordinating the personal life to the creation of a world directorate capable of these tasks and to the general advancement of human knowledge, capacity and power.

The admission therewith that our immortality is conditional and lies in the race and not in our individual selves.

CHAPTER XIII

EARLY CONSTRUCTIVE WORK
OF THE OPEN CONSPIRACY

In such terms we may sketch the practicable and possible opening phase of the Open Conspiracy.

We do not present it as a movement initiated by any individual or radiating from any particular centre. It arises naturally and necessarily from the present increase of knowledge and the broadening outlook of many minds throughout the world. It is reasonable therefore to anticipate its appearance all over the world in sporadic mutually independent groups and to recognise not only that they will be extremely various but that many of them will trail with them racial and regional habits and characteristics which will only be shaken off as its cosmopolitan character becomes imperatively evident. The passage from the partial anticipations of the Open Conspiracy that already abound everywhere to its complete and completely self-conscious statement may be made by almost imperceptible degrees. To-day it may seem no more than a visionary idea ; to-morrow it may be realised as a world-wide force of opinion and will. People will pass with no great inconsistency from saying that the Open Conspiracy is impossible to saying that it has always been plain and clear to them, that to this fashion they have shaped their lives as long as they can remember.

In its opening phase, in the day of small things, quite minor accidents may help or delay the clear definition and popularisation of its main ideas. The changing pattern· of public events may disperse or concentrate attention upon it, or it may win the early adherence of men of exceptional resources, energy or ability. It is impossible to foretell the speed of its advance. Its development may be slower or faster, direct or devious, but the logic of accumulating realisations thrusts it forward, will persist in thrusting it on, and sooner or later it will be discovered, conscious and potent, the working religion of most sane and energetic people.

Meanwhile our supreme virtues must be faith and persistence.

So far we have considered only two of the main activities of the Open Conspiracy, the one being its propaganda of confidence in the possible world commonweal and the other its immediate practical attempt to systematise resistance to militant and competitive imperialism and nationalism. But such things are merely its groundwork undertakings ; they do no more than clear the site and make the atmosphere possible for its organised constructive efforts.

Directly we turn to that we turn to questions of special knowledge, special effort and special organisation.

Let us consider first the general advancement of science, the protection and support of scientific research and the diffusion of scientific knowledge.

These things fall within the normal scheme of duty for the members of the Open Conspiracy. The world of science and experiment is the region of origin of nearly all the great initiatives that characterise our times ; the Open Conspiracy owes its inspiration, its existence, its form and direction entirely to the changes of condition these initiatives have brought about, and yet a large number of scientific workers live outside the sphere of sympathy in which we may expect the Open Conspiracy to materialise, and collectively their political and social influence upon the community is extraordinarily small. Having regard to the immensity of its contributions and the incalculable value of its promise to the modern community, science—research, that is, and the diffusion of scientific knowledge—is extraordinarily neglected, starved and threatened by hostile interference. This is largely because it has no strong unifying organisation and cannot in itself develop such an organisation.

Science is a hard mistress and the first condition of successful scientific work is that the scientific man should stick to his research. The world of science is therefore in itself, at its core, a miscellany of specialists, often very ungracious specialists, and, rather than offer him help and co-operation, it calls for understanding, tolerance and service from the man of more general intelligence and wider purpose. The company of scientific men is less like a host of guiding angels than like a swarm of marvellous bees —endowed with stings—which must be hived and cherished and multiplied by the Open Conspiracy.

But so soon as we have the Open Conspiracy at work, putting its case plainly and offering its developing organisation to those most preciously preoccupied men, then reasonably, when it involves no special trouble for them, when it is the line of least resistance for them, they may be expected to fall in with its convenient and helpful ideas, and find in it what they have hitherto lacked, a common system of political and social concepts to hold them together. When that stage is reached, we shall be saved such spectacles of intellectual prostitution as the last Great War offered, when men of science were herded blinking from their laboratories to curse one another upon nationalist lines, and when after the war stupid and wicked barriers were set up to the free communication of knowledge by the exclusion of scientific men of this or that nationality from international scientific gatherings. The Open Conspiracy must help the man of science to realise, what at present he fails most astonishingly to realise, that he belongs to a greater comity than any king or president represents to-day, and so prepare him for better behaviour in the next season of trial.

The formation of groups in, and not only in, but about and in relation to, the scientific world, which will add to those first main activities of the Open Conspiracy, propaganda and pacificism, a special attention to the needs of scientific work, may be enlarged upon with advantage here, because it will illustrate quite typically the idea of a special work carried on in relation to a general activity, which is the subject of this section.

The Open Conspiracy extends its invitation to all

sorts and conditions of men, but the service of scientific progress is for those only who are specially equipped or who are sufficiently interested to equip themselves. For scientific work there is first of all a great need of endowment and the setting up of laboratories, observatories, experimental stations and the like in all parts of the world. Numbers of men and women capable of scientific work never achieve it for want of the stimulus of opportunity afforded by endowment. Few contrive to create their own opportunities. The essential man of science is very rarely an able collector or administrator of money and anyhow the detailed work of organisation is a grave call upon his special mental energy. But many men capable of a broad and intelligent appreciation of scientific work, but not capable of the peculiar intensities of research, have the gift of extracting money from private and public sources, and it is for them to use that gift modestly and generously in providing the framework for those more especially endowed.

And there is already a steadily increasing need for the proper storage and indexing of scientific results, and every fresh worker enhances it. Quite a considerable amount of scientific work goes fruitless or is needlessly repeated, because of the growing volume of publication, and men make discoveries in the field of reality only to lose them again in the lumber-room of record. Here is a second line of activity to which the Open Conspirator with a scientific bias may direct his attention.

A third line is the liaison work between the man of science and the common intelligent man ; the

promotion of publications which will either state
the substance, implications and consequences of new
work in the vulgar tongue, or, if that is impossible,
train the general run of people to the new idioms
and technicalities which need to be incorporated
with the vulgar tongue if it is still to serve its ends as
a means of intellectual intercourse.

Through special *ad hoc* organisations, societies for
the promotion of Research, for Research Defence,
for World Indexing, for the translation of Scientific
Papers, for the Diffusion of New Knowledge, the
surplus energies of a great number of Open Conspirators can be directed to entirely creative ends
and a new world organisation of scientific work
built up, within which such dear old institutions as
the Royal Society of London, the various European
Academies of Science and the like, now overgrown
and inadequate, can maintain their venerable pride
in themselves, their mellowing prestige and their
distinguished exclusiveness, without their present
privilege of inflicting cramping slights and restrictions
upon the more abundant scientific activities of to-day.

So in relation to Science—and here the word is
being used in its narrower accepted meaning for
what is often spoken of as *pure* science, the search for
physical and biological realities, uncomplicated by
moral, social and " practical " considerations—we
evoke a conception of the Open Conspiracy as producing groups of socially associated individuals,
who engage primarily in the general basic activities
of the Conspiracy and adhere to and promote the
six broad principles summarised at the end of Chapter
Twelve, but who work also with the larger part of

their energies, through international and cosmopolitan societies and in a multitude of special
ways, for the establishment of an enduring and
progressive world organisation of pure research.
They will have come to this special work because
their distinctive gifts, their inclinations, their
positions and opportunities have indicated it as
theirs.

Now a very parallel system of Open Conspiracy
groups is conceivable, in relation to business and
industrial life. It would necessarily be a vastly
bulkier and more heterogeneous system of groups
but otherwise the analogy is complete. Here we
imagine those people whose gifts, inclinations,
positions and opportunities as directors, workers or
associates give them an exceptional insight into and
influence in the processes of producing and distribu-
ting commodities, can also be drawn together into
groups within the Open Conspiracy. But these
groups will be concerned with the huge and more
complicated problems of the processes by which
even now the small isolated individual adventures
in production and trading, that constituted the
economic life of former civilisations, are giving place
to larger, better instructed, better planned industrial
organisations, whose operations and combinations
become at last world wide.

The amalgamations and combinations, the substi-
tution of large-scale business for multitudes of small-
scale businesses, which are going on now, go on with
all the cruelty and disregards of a natural process.
If man is to profit and survive, these unconscious
blunderings—which now stagger towards but which

may never attain world organisation—must be watched, controlled, mastered and directed. As uncertainty diminishes, the quality of adventure and the amount of waste diminish also, and large speculative profits are no longer possible or justifiable. The transition from speculative adventure to organised foresight in the common interest, in the whole world of economic life, is the substantial task of the Open Conspiracy. And it is these specially interested and equipped groups and not the movement as a whole which may best begin the attack upon these fundamental readjustments.

The various Socialist movements of the nineteenth and earlier twentieth centuries had this in common, that they sought to replace the " private owner " in most or all economic interests by some vaguely apprehended " public owner." This, following the democratic disposition of the times, was commonly conceived of as an elected body, a municipality, the parliamentary state or what not. There were municipal socialists, " nationalising " socialists, imperial socialists. In the mystic teachings of the Marxist, the collective owner was to be " the dictatorship of the proletariat." Production for profit was denounced. The contemporary mind realises the evils of production for profit and of the indiscriminate scrambling of private ownership, but it has a completer realisation and a certain accumulation of experience of the difficulties of organising that larger ownership we desire. Private ownership may not be altogether evil as a provisional stage even if it has no more in its favour than the ability to transcend political boundaries.

Moreover—and here again the democratic prepossessions of the nineteenth century come in—the Socialist movements sought to make every single adherent a reformer and a propagandist of economic methods. In order to do so, it was necessary to simplify economic processes to the crudity of nursery toys, and the intricate interplay of will and desire in enterprise, normal employment and direction, in questions of ownership, wages, credit and money, was reduced to a childish fable of surplus value wickedly appropriated. The Open Conspiracy is not so much a socialism as a more comprehensive scheme that has eaten and assimilated whatever was digestible of its socialist forebears. It turns to biology for guidance towards the regulation of quantity and a controlled distribution of the human population of the world, and it judges all the subsidiary aspects of property and pay by the criterion of most efficient production and distribution in relation to the indications thus obtained.

These economic groups, then, of the Open Conspiracy, which may come indeed to be a large part of the Open Conspiracy, will be working in that vast task of economic reconstruction—which from the point of view of the older socialism was the sole task before mankind. They will be conducting experiments and observing processes according to their opportunities. Through *ad hoc* societies and journals they will be comparing and examining their methods and preparing reports and clear information for the movement at large. The whole question of money and monetary methods in our modern communities, so extraordinarily disregarded in socialist literature, will be examined under the assumption that money is the token of the community's obligation, direct or indirect, to an individual, and credit its permission to deal freely with material.

The whole psychology of industry and industrial relationship needs to be revised and restated in terms of the collective efficiency and welfare of mankind. And just as far as can be contrived, the counsel and the confidences of those who now direct great industrial and financial operations will be invoked. The first special task of a banker, or a bank clerk for that matter, who joins the Open Conspiracy, will be to answer the questions : " What is a bank ? " " What are you going to do about it ? " " What have we to do about it ? " The first question to a manufacturer will be : " What are you making and why ? " and " What are you and we to do about it ? " Instead of the crude proposals to " expropriate " and " take over by the state " of the primitive socialism, the Open Conspiracy will build up an encyclopædic conception of the modern economic complex as a labyrinthine pseudo-system progressively eliminating waste and working its way along multitudinous channels towards unity, towards clarity of purpose and method, towards abundant productivity and efficient social service.

Let us come back now for a paragraph or so to the ordinary adherent to the Open Conspiracy, the adherent considered not in relation to his special aptitudes and services, but in relation to the movement as a whole and to those special constructive organisations outside his own field. It will be his duty to keep his mind in touch with the progressing concepts of the scientific work so far as he is able and with the larger issues of the economic reconstruction that is afoot, to take his cues from the special groups and organisations engaged upon that work, and to help where he finds his opportunity and when there is a call upon him. But no adherent of the Open Conspiracy can remain merely and completely an ordinary adherent. There can be no pawns in the game of the Open Conspiracy, no " cannon fodder " in its war. A special activity quite as much as a general understanding is demanded from everyone who looks creatively towards the future of mankind.

We have instanced first the fine and distinctive world organisation of pure science and then the huge massive movement towards co-operating unity of aim in the economic life until at last the production and distribution of staple necessities is apprehended as one world business, and we have suggested that this latter movement may gradually pervade and incorporate a very great bulk of human activities. But besides this fine current and this great torrent of evolving activities and relationships there are also a very considerable variety of other great functions in the community towards which Open Conspiracy groups must direct their organising enquiries and suggestions in their common intention of ultimately assimilating all the confused processes of to-day into a world community.

For example, there must be a series of groups in close touch at one end with biological science and at the other with the complex of economic activity, who will be concerned specially with the practical administration of the biological interests of the race, from food-plants and industrial products to pestilences and population. And another series of groups will gather together attention and energy to focus them upon the educational process. We have already pointed out in Chapter Nine that there is a strong disposition towards conservatism in normal educational institutions. They preserve traditions rather than develop them. They are likely to set up a considerable resistance to the reconstruction of the world outlook upon the threefold basis defined in Chapter Twelve. This resistance must be attacked by special societies, by the establishment of competing schools, by help and promotion for enlightened teachers, and, wherever the attack is incompletely successful, it must be supplemented by the energetic diffusion of educational literature for adults, upon modern lines. The forces of the entire movement may be mobilised in a variety of ways to bring pressure upon reactionary schools and institutions.

A set of activities correlated with most of the directly creative ones will lie through existing political and administrative bodies. The political work of the Open Conspiracy must be conducted upon two levels and by entirely different methods. Its main political idea, its political strategy, is to weaken, efface, incorporate or supersede existing governments. But there is also a tactical diversion of administrative powers and resources to economic and educational arrangements of a modern type. Because a country or a district is inconvenient as a division and destined to ultimate absorption in some more comprehensive and economical system of government, that is no reason why its administration should not be brought meanwhile into working co-operation with the development of the Open Conspiracy. Free Trade nationalism in power is better than high tariff nationalism, and pacificist party liberalism better than aggressive party patriotism.

This evokes the anticipation of another series of groups, a group in every possible political division, whose task it will be to organise the whole strength of the Open Conspiracy in that division as an effective voting or agitating force. In many divisions this might soon become a sufficiently considerable block to affect the attitudes and pledges of the national politicians. The organisation of these political groups into provincial or national conferences and systems would follow hard upon their appearance. In their programmes they would be guided by meetings and discussions with the specifically economic, educational, biological, scientific and central groups, but they would also form their own special research bodies to work out the incessant problems of transition between the old type of locally centred administrations and a developing world system of political controls.

In the preceding chapter we sketched the first practicable first phase of the Open Conspiracy as the propaganda of a group of interlocking ideas, a propaganda associated with pacificist action. In the present chapter we have given a scheme of branching and amplifying development. In this scheme, this scheme of the second phase, we conceive of the Open Conspiracy as consisting of a great multitude and variety of overlapping groups, but now all organised for collective political, social and educational as well as propagandist action. They will recognise each other much more clearly than they did at first and they will have acquired a common name.

The groups, however, almost all of them, will still have specific work also. Some will be organising a sounder setting for scientific progress, some exploring new social and educational possibilities, many concentrated upon this or that phase in the re-organisation of the world's economic life and so forth. The individual Open Conspirator may belong to one or more groups and in addition to the *ad hoc* societies and organisations which the movement will sustain, often in co-operation with partially sympathetic people still outside its ranks.

The character of the Open Conspiracy will now be plainly displayed. It will have become a great world movement as widespread and evident as socialism or communism. It will largely have taken the place of these movements. It will be more, it will be a world religion. This large loose assimilatory mass of groups and societies will be definitely and obviously attempting to swallow up the entire population of the world and become the new human community.

CHAPTER XIV

EXISTING AND DEVELOPING MOVEMENTS WITH WHICH THE OPEN CONSPIRACY MAY HOPE TO COALESCE

A suggestion has already been made in an earlier chapter of this essay which may perhaps be expanded here a little more. It is that there already exist in the world a considerable number of movements in industry, in political life, in social matters, in education, which point in the same direction as the Open Conspiracy. It will be interesting to discuss how far some of these movements may not become confluent with others and by a mere process of logical completion identify themselves with the Open Conspiracy.

Consider, for example, the movement for a scientific study and control of population pressure, known popularly as the Birth Control Movement. By itself, assuming existing political and economic conditions, this movement lays itself open to the charge of being no better than a scheme of " race suicide." If a population in some area of high civilisation attempts to restrict increase, organise its economic life upon methods of maximum individual productivity and impose order and beauty upon its entire territory, that region will become irresistibly

Ic

attractive to any adjacent festering mass of low-grade highly reproductive population. The cheap humanity of the one community will make a constant attack upon the other, affording facile servility, prostitutes, toilers, hand labour. Tariffs against sweated products, restriction of immigration, tensions leading at last to a war of defensive massacre are inevitable. The conquest of an illiterate, hungry and incontinent multitude may be almost as disastrous as defeat for the selecter race. Indeed one finds that in discussion the propagandists of Birth Control admit that their project must be universal or dysgenic. But yet quite a number of them do not follow up these admissions to their logical consequences, produce the lines and continue the curves until the complete form of the Open Conspiracy appears. It will be the business of the early Open Conspiracy propagandists to make them do so, and to install groups and representatives at every possible point of vantage in this movement.

And similarly the now very numerous associations for world peace halt in alarm on the edge of their own implications. World Peace remains a vast aspiration until there is some substitute for the present competition of states for markets and raw material, and some restraint upon population pressure. League of Nations Societies and all forms of pacificist organisation are either futile or insincere until they come into line with the complementary propositions of the Open Conspiracy.

The various socialist movements again are partial projects professing at present to be self-sufficient schemes. Most of them involve a pretence that national and political forces are intangible phantoms and that the primary issue of population pressure can be ignored. They produce one woolly scheme after another for transferring the property in this, that or the other economic plant and interest from bodies of shareholders and company promoters to gangs of politicians or to syndicates of workers— to be steered to efficiency, it would seem, by pillars of cloud by day and pillars of fire by night. The communist party has trained a whole generation of disciples to believe that the overthrow of a vaguely apprehended " Capitalism " is the simple solution of all human difficulties. No movement ever succeeded so completely in substituting phrases for thought. In Moscow communism has trampled " Capitalism " underfoot for ten eventful years, and still finds all the problems of social and political construction before it.

But as soon as the Socialist or Communist can be got to realise that his repudiation of private monopolisation is not a complete programme but just a preliminary principle, he is ripe for the ampler concepts of the modern outlook. The Open Conspiracy is the natural inheritor of socialist and communist enthusiasms ; it may be in control of Moscow before it is in control of New York.

The Open Conspiracy may achieve the more or less complete amalgamation of all the radical impulses in the Atlantic community of to-day. But its scope is not confined to the variety of sympathetic movements which are brought to mind by that loose word *radical*. In the past fifty years or so while Socialists and Communists have been denouncing the

current processes of economic life in the same invariable phrases and with the same undiscriminating
animosity, these processes have been undergoing the
profoundest and most interesting changes. While
socialist thought has recited its phrases, with witty
rather than substantial variations, a thousand times
as many clever people have been busy upon industrial,
mercantile and financial processes. The Socialist
still reiterates that this greater body of intelligence
has been merely seeking private gain, which has just
as much truth in it as is necessary to make it an
intoxicating lie. Everywhere competitive businesses
have been giving way to amalgamated enterprises,
marching towards monopoly, and personally owned
businesses to organisations so large as to acquire
more and more the character of publicly responsible
bodies. In theory in Great Britain, banks are
privately owned and railway transport is privately
owned, and they are run entirely for profit—in
practice their profit making is austerely restrained
and their proceedings are all the more sensitive to
public welfare because they are outside the direct
control of party politicians.

Now this transformation of business, trading and
finance has been so multitudinous and so rapid as to
be still largely unconscious of itself. Intelligent
men have gone from combination to combination
and extended their range, year by year, without
realising how their activities were enlarging them to
conspicuousness and responsibility. Economic organisation is even now only discovering itself for what it
is. It has accepted incompatible existing institutions
to its own great injury. It has been patriotic and

broken its shins against the tariff walls its patriotism has raised to hamper its own movements ; it has been imperial and found itself taxed to the limits of its endurance, " controlled " by antiquated military and naval experts and crippled altogether. The younger, more vigorous intelligences in the great business directorates of to-day are beginning to realise the uncompleted implications of their enterprise. A day will come when the gentlemen who are trying to control the oil supplies of the world without reference to anything else except as a subsidiary factor in their game, will be considered to be quaint characters. The ends of Big Business must carry Big Business into the Open Conspiracy, just as surely as every other creative and broadly organising movement is carried.

Now I know that to all this urging towards a unification of constructive effort, a great number of people will be disposed to a reply which will, I hope, be less popular in the future than it is at the present time. They will assume first an expression of great sagacity, an elderly air. Then, smiling gently, they will ask whether there is not something preposterously ambitious in looking at the problem of life as one whole. Is it not wiser to concentrate our forces on more *practicable* things, to attempt one thing at a time, not to antagonise the whole order of established things against our poor desires, to begin tentatively to refrain from putting too great a strain upon people, to trust to the growing common sense of the world to adjust this or that line of progress to the general scheme of things. Far better accomplish something definite here and there than challenge a general failure. That is, they declare, how reformers and creative things have gone on in the past ; that is how they are going on now ; muddling forward in a mild and confused and partially successful way. Why not trust them to go on like that ? Let each man do his bit with a complete disregard of the logical interlocking of progressive effort to which I have been drawing attention.

Now I must confess that, popular as this style of argument is, it gives me so tedious a feeling that rather than argue against it in general terms I will resort to a parable. I will relate the story of the pig on Provinder Island.

There was, you must understand, only one pig on Provinder Island, and Heaven knows how it got there, whether it escaped and swam ashore or was put ashore from some vessel suddenly converted to vegetarianism, I cannot imagine. At first it was the only mammal there. But later on three sailors and a very small but observant cabin-boy were wrecked there, and after subsisting for a time on shell-fish and roots they became aware of this pig. And simultaneously they became aware of a nearly intolerable craving for bacon. The eldest of the three sailors began to think of a ham he had met in his boyhood, a beautiful ham for which his father had had the carving knife specially sharpened ; the second of the three sailors dreamed repeatedly of a roast loin of pork he had eaten at his sister's wedding, and the third's mind ran on chitterlings—I know not why. They sat about their meagre fire and conferred and expatiated upon these things until their mouths watered and the shell-fish turned to water within them. What dreams came to the cabin-boy are unknown, for it was their custom to discourage his confidences. But he sat apart brooding and was at last moved to speech. " Let us hunt that old pig," he said, " and kill it."

Now it may have been because it was the habit of these sailors to discourage the cabin-boy and keep him in his place, but anyhow, for whatever reason it was, all three sailors set themselves with one accord to oppose that proposal.

" Who spoke of killing the pig ? " said the eldest sailor loudly, looking round to see if by any chance the pig was within hearing. " Who spoke of *killing* the pig ? You're the sort of silly young devil who jumps at ideas and hasn't no sense of difficulties. What I said was *AM*. All I want is just a Am to go with my roots and sea salt. One Am. The Left Am. I don't want the right one and I don't propose to get it. I've got a sense of proportion and a proper share of humour and I know my limitations. I'm a sound clear-headed practical man. Am is what I'm after, and if I can get that, I'm prepared to say Quits and let the rest of the pig alone. Who's for joining me in a Left Am Unt—a simple reasonable Left Am Unt— just to get One Left Am ? "

Nobody answered him directly, but when his voice died away, the next sailor in order of seniority took up the tale. " That Boy," he said, " will die of Swelled Ed, and I pity im. My idea is to follow up the pig and get hold of a loin chop. Just simply a loin chop. A loin chop is good enough for me. It's— feasible. Much more feasible than a great Am. Here we are, we've not no gun, we've got no wood of a sort to make bows and arrows, we've not nothing but our clasp knives, and that pig can run like Ell. It's ridiculous to think of killing that pig. But if one didn't trouble him, if one kind of got into his confidence and crept near him and just quietly and insidiously went for his loin—just sort of as if one was tickling him—one might get a loin chop almost before he knew of it."

The third sailor sat crumpled up and downcast with his lean fingers tangled in his shock of hair. " Chitterlings," he murmured, " chitterlings. I don't even want to *think* of the pig."

And the cabin-boy pursued his own ideas in silence, for he deemed it unwise to provoke his elders further.

On these lines it was the three sailors set about the gratifying of their taste for pork, each in his own way, separately and sanely and modestly. And each had his reward. The first sailor after weeks of patience got within arm's length of the pig and smacked that coveted left ham loud and good, and felt success was near. The other two heard the smack and the grunt of dismay half a mile away. But the pig in a state of astonishment carried the ham off out of reach, there and then, and that was as close as the first sailor ever got to his objective. The roast loin hunter did no better. He came upon the pig asleep under a rock one day, and jumped upon the very loin he desired, but the pig bit him deeply and septically, and displayed so much resentment that the question of a chop was dropped forthwith and never again broached between them. And thereafter the arm of the second sailor was bandaged and swelled up and went from bad to worse. And as for the third sailor, it is doubtful whether he even got wind of a chitterling from the start to the finish of this parable. The cabin-boy pursuing notions of his own made a pitfall for the whole pig, but as the others did not help him, and as he was an excessively small—though shrewd—cabin-boy, it was a feeble and insufficient pitfall and all it caught was the hunter of chitterlings who was wandering distraught. After which the hunter of chitterlings became a hunter of cabin-boys, and the cabin-boy's life, for all his shrewdness, was precarious and unpleasant. He slept only in snatches and learned the full bitterness of insight misunderstood.

When at last a ship came to Provinder Island and took off the three men and the cabin-boy, the pig was still bacon intact and quite gay and cheerful, and all four castaways were in a very emaciated condition because at that season of the year shell-fish were rare and edible roots were hard to find and the pig was very much cleverer than they were in finding them and digging them up—let alone digesting them.

From which parable it may be gathered that a partial enterprise is not always wiser or more hopeful than a comprehensive one.

And in the same manner, with myself in the rôle of that minute but observant cabin-boy, I would sustain the proposition that none of these movements of partial reconstruction has the sound common-sense quality its supporters suppose. All these movements are worth while if they can be taken into a world-wide movement ; all in isolation are futile.

They will be overlaid and lost in the general drift. The policy of the whole hog is the best one, the sanest one, the easiest and the most hopeful. If sufficient men and women of intelligence can realise that simple truth and give up their lives to it, mankind may yet achieve a civilisation and power and fullness of life beyond our present dreams. If they do not, frustration will triumph, and war, violence and a drivelling waste of time and strength and desire, more disgusting even than war, will be the lot of our race down through the ages to its emaciated and miserable end.

For this little planet of ours is quite off the course of any rescue ships, if the will in our species fails.

CHAPTER XV

THE CREATIVE HOME, SOCIAL GROUP AND SCHOOL: THE PRESENT WASTE OF YOUTHFUL SERIOUSNESS

Human society began with the family. The natural history of gregariousness is a history of the establishment of mutual toleration among human animals, so that a litter or a herd keeps together instead of breaking up. It is in the family group that the restraints, disciplines and self-sacrifices which make human society possible were worked out and our fundamental prejudices established, and it is in the family group that our social life must be relearnt generation after generation.

Now in each generation the Open Conspiracy must remain a minority movement of intelligent converts until it can develop its own reproductive methods. A unified progressive world community demands its own type of home and training. It needs to have its fundamental concepts firmly established in as many minds as possible and to guard its children from the infection of the old racial and national hatreds and jealousies, old superstitions and bad mental habits, and base interpretations of life. From its outset the Open Conspiracy will be setting itself to influence the existing educational machinery, but for a long time it will find itself confronted in school and college by powerful religious and political authorities determined to set back the children at the point or even behind the point from which their parents made their escape. At best, the liberalism of the state-controlled schools will be a compromise. During the early phases of its struggle, therefore, the Open Conspiracy will be obliged to adopt a certain sectarianism of domestic and social life in the interests of its children, and it may even in many cases have to consider the grouping of its families and the establishment of its own schools. In many modern communities, the English-speaking states, for example, there is still liberty to establish educational companies, running schools of a special type. In every country where that right does not exist it has to be fought for.

There lies a great work for various groups of the Open Conspiracy. Successful schools would become laboratories of educational methods and patterns for the state schools. Necessarily for a time, the Open Conspiracy children would become a social élite; from their first conscious moments they would begin to think and talk among clear-headed people speaking distinctly and behaving frankly, and it would be a waste and loss to put them back for the scholastic stage among their mentally indistinct and morally muddled contemporaries. A phase when there will be a special educational system for the Open Conspiracy is, therefore, clearly indicated. Its children will learn to speak, draw, think, compute lucidly and subtly, and into their vigorous minds they will take the broad concepts of history, biology and mechanical progress, the basis of the new world, naturally and easily. Meanwhile, those who grow up outside the advancing educational frontier of the Open Conspiracy will never come under the full influence of its ideas, or they will get hold of them only after a severe struggle against a mass of mis-representations and elaborately instilled prejudices.

The Open Conspiracy will not be in health until it has segregated its home life and much of its social life from the general confusions of to-day, until its adherents marry and associate preferentially within the movement and keep themselves essentially aloof from the prevalent methods of wasting time and interest. They must evolve a new social atmosphere. It will be a minor aspect of the world revolution to live down the contemporary theatre, contemporary " amusements," the sentimental booms and imita-tive chatter, the ovine congregating to gape at this or that, the dull pursuit of sports and " games " and quasi-innocent vices, the fashions and industrious futilities of current life so soon as it escapes from poverty. The whole drift of the contemporary world is to tempt and ensnare and waste our children. It has a diabolical disposition to make life altogether trivial and ineffective. Over all these matters women seem to have much more aptitude and power than men. It may not be true that " woman's sphere is the home," but certainly the home and its immediate social atmosphere is her empire. She can be the moral quite as much as the physical mother of the days to come.

Always, as long as I can remember, there has been a dispute and invidious comparisons between the

old and the young. The young find the old prey upon
and restrain them and the old find the young, shal-
low, disappointing and aimless in vivid contrast to
their own revised memories of their own early days.
The present time is one in which these perennial
accusations flower with exceptional vigour. But
there does seem to be some truth in the statement
that the facilities to live frivolously are greater now
than they have ever been for old and young alike.
In the great communities that emerge from Christendom, there is a widespread disposition to regard
Sunday as merely a holiday. But that was certainly
not the original intention of Sunday. As we have
noted already in an earlier chapter, it was
a day dedicated to the greater issues of life. Now
great multitudes of people do not even pretend to set
aside any time at all to the greater issues of life. The
churches are neglected and nothing of a unifying
or exalting sort takes their place.

Now what the contemporary senior tells his junior
to-day is perfectly correct. In his youth, no serious
impulse of his went to waste. He was not distracted
by a thousand gay but petty temptations, and the
local religious powers, whatever they happened to
be, seemed to believe in themselves more and made
a more comprehensive attack upon his conscience
and imagination. Now the old faiths are damaged
and discredited and the new and greater one, which
is the Open Conspiracy, takes shape only slowly. A
decade or so ago, socialism preached its confident
hopes, and patriotism and imperial pride shared its
attraction for the ever grave and passionate will of
emergent youth. Now socialism and democracy are

" under revision " and the flags that once waved so bravely reek of poison gas, are stiff with blood and mud and shameful with exposed dishonesties. Youth is what youth has always been, eager for fine inter-pretations of life, capable of splendid resolves. But it comes up out of its childhood to-day into a world of ruthless exposures and cynical pretensions. The past ten years has seen the shy and powerful idealism of youth at a loss and dismayed as perhaps it has never been before. It is in the world still, but masked, hiding even from itself in a whirl of small excitements and futile defiant depravities.

The old flags and faiths have lost their magic for the intelligence of the young ; they can command it no more ; it is in the mighty revolution to which the Open Conspiracy directs itself that the youth of mankind must once more find its soul if ever it is to find its soul again.

CHAPTER XVI

PROGRESSIVE DEVELOPMENT OF THE ACTIVITIES OF THE OPEN CONSPIRACY INTO A WORLD CONTROL AND COMMON-WEAL : THE HAZARDS OF THE CONFLICT

We have now sketched out in these Blue Prints, the methods by which the confused radicalism and constructive forces of the present time may and can and probably will be drawn together about a core of modernised religious feeling into one great and multifarious creative effort. A way has been shown by which this effort may be developed from a mere propagandist campaign and a merely resistant protest against contemporary militarism into an organised foreshadowing in research, publicity and experiment in educational, economic and political reconstructions, of that *Pax Mundi*, which has be-come already the tantalised desire of great multitudes throughout the world. These foreshadowings and reconstructions will ignore and transcend the political boundaries of to-day. They will continually become more substantial as project passes into at-tempt and performance. In phase after phase and at point after point, therefore, the Open Conspiracy will come to grips with the powers that sustain these boundaries.

And it will not be merely topographical boundaries that will be passed. The Open Conspiracy will
also be dissolving and repudiating many existing
restrictions upon conduct and many social prejudices.
The Open Conspiracy proposes to end and shows
how an end may be put to that huge substratum of
under-developed, under-educated, subjugated, exploited and frustrated lives upon which such civilisation as the world has known hitherto has rested,
and upon which most of our social systems still rest.

Whenever possible, the Open Conspiracy will
advance by illumination and persuasion. But it has
to advance and even from the outset where it is not
allowed to illuminate and persuade it must fight. Its
first fights will probably be for the right to spread its
system of ideas plainly and clearly throughout the
world.

There is, I suppose, a flavour of treason about the
assumption that any established government is
provisional, and a quality of immorality in any criticism of accepted moral standards. Still more is the
proposal, made even in times of peace, to resist war
levies and conscription, an offence against absolute
conceptions of loyalty. But the ampler wisdom of the
modern Atlantic communities, already touched by
premonitions of change and futurity, has continually enlarged the common liberties of thought for
some generations, and it is doubtful if there will be
any serious resistance to the dissemination of these
views and the early organisation of the Open Conspiracy in any of the English-speaking communities
or throughout the British Empire, in the Scandinavian
countries, or in such liberal-minded countries as

Kc

Holland, Switzerland, republican Germany or France. France, in the hasty years after the war, submitted to some repressive legislation against the discussion of birth control or hostile criticism of the militarist attitude ; but such a check upon mental freedom is altogether contrary to the clear and open quality of the French mind ; in practice it has already been effectively repudiated by such writers as Victor Margueritte, and it is unlikely that there will be any effective suppression of the opening phases of the Open Conspiracy in France.

This gives us a large portion of the existing civilised world in which men's minds may be readjusted to the idea that their existing governments are in the position of trustees for the greater government of the coming age. Throughout these communities it is conceivable that the structural lines of the world community may be materialised and established with only minor struggles, local boycotts, vigorous public controversies, normal legislative obstruction, social pressure and overt political activities. Police, jail, expulsions and so forth, let alone outlawry and warfare, may scarcely be brought into this struggle upon the high civilised level of the Atlantic communities. But where they are brought in, the Open Conspiracy to the best of its ability and the full extent of its resources, must become a fighting force and organise itself upon resistant lines.

Non-resistance, the restriction of activities to moral suasion, is no part of the programme of the Open Conspiracy. In the face of unscrupulous opposition creative ideas must become aggressive, must define their enemies and attack them. By its own organisations or through the police and military strength of governments amenable to its ideas, the movement is bound to find itself fighting for open roads, open frontiers, freedom of speech and the realities of peace in regions of oppression. The Open Conspiracy rests upon a disrespect for nationality and there is no reason why it should tolerate noxious or obstructive governments because they hold their own in this or that patch of human territory. It lies within the power of the Atlantic communities to impose peace upon the world and secure un-impeded movement and free speech from end to end of the earth. This is a fact on which the Open Con-spiracy must insist. The English-speaking states, France, Germany, Holland, Swtizerland, the Scan-dinavian countries and Russia, given only a not very extravagant frankness of understanding between them, and a common disposition towards the ideas of the Open Conspiracy, could cease to arm against each other and still exert enough strength to impose disarmament and a respect for human freedom in every corner of the planet. It is fantastic pedantry to wait for all the world to accede before all the world is pacified and policed.

The most inconsistent factor in the liberal and radical thought of to-day is its prejudice against the interference of highly developed modern states in the affairs of less stable and less advanced regions. This is denounced as " imperialism," and regarded as criminal. It may have assumed grotesque and dangerous forms under the now dying traditions of national competition, but as the merger of the Atlantic states proceeds, the possibility and necessity of bringing areas of misgovernment and disorder under world control increase. A great war like the war of 1914–1918 may never happen again. The common-sense of mankind may suffice to avert that. But there is still much actual warfare before mankind, on the frontiers everywhere, against brigands, against ancient loyalties and traditions which will become at last no better than excuses for brigandage and obstructive exaction. All the weight of the Open Conspiracy will be on the side of the world order and against that sort of local independence which holds back its subject people from the citizenship of the world.

But in this broad prospect of far-reaching political amalgamations under the impulses of the Open Conspiracy lurk a thousand antagonisms and adverse chances, like the unsuspected gulleys and ravines and thickets in a wide and distant landscape. We know not what unexpected chasms may presently be discovered. The Open Conspirator may realise that he is one of an advancing and victorious force and still find himself outnumbered and outfought in his own particular corner of the battlefield. No one can yet estimate the possible strength of reaction against world unification ; no one can foresee the extent of the divisions and confusions that may arise among ourselves. The ideas in this book may be spread about without any serious resistance in most civilised countries, but there are still governments under which the persistent expression of such thoughts will be dealt with as crimes and bring men and women to prison, torment and death. Nevertheless they must be expressed.

While the Open Conspiracy is no more than a discussion it may spread unopposed because it is disregarded. As a mainly passive resistance to militarism it may still be tolerable. But as its knowledge and experience accumulate and its organisation becomes more effective and aggressive, as it begins to lay hands upon education, upon social habits, upon business developments, as it proceeds to take over the organisation of the community, it will marshal not only its own forces but its enemies. A complex of interests will find themselves restrained and threatened by it and it may easily evoke that most dangerous of human mass feelings, fear. In ways quite unpredictable it may raise a storm against itself beyond all our present imaginings. Our conception of an almost bloodless domination of the Atlantic communities may be merely the confident dream of a thinker whose thoughts have yet to be squarely challenged.

We are not even sure of the common peace. Across the path of mankind the storm of another Great War may break, bringing with it for a time more brutal repressions and vaster injuries even than its predecessor. The scaffoldings and work-sheds of the Open Conspiracy may fare violently in that tornado. The restoration of progress may seem an almost hopeless struggle.

It is no part of the modern religion to incur needless hardship or go out of the way to seek martyrdom. If we can do our work easily and happily, so it should be done. But the work is not to be shirked because it cannot be done easily and happily. The vision of a world at peace and liberated for an unending growth of knowledge and power is worth every danger of the way. And since in this age of confusion we must live imperfectly and anyhow die, we may as well suffer if need be, and die for a great end as for none. Never has the translation of vision into realities been easy since the beginning of human effort. The establishment of the world community will surely exact a price—and who can tell what that price may be?—in toil, suffering and blood.

CHAPTER XVII

THE WORLD COMMUNITY

The new life that the Open Conspiracy struggles to achieve through us for our race is first a life of liberations. The oppression of incessant toil can surely be lifted from everyone, and the miseries due to a great multitude of infections and disorders of nutrition and growth cease to be a part of human experience. Few people are perfectly healthy nowadays except for brief periods of happiness, but the elation of physical well-being will some day be the common lot of mankind. And not only from natural evils will man be largely free. He will not be left with his soul tangled, haunted by monstrous and irrational fears and a prey to malicious impulse. From his birth he will breathe sweetness and generosity and use his mind and hands cleanly and exactly. He will feel better, will better, think better, see, taste and hear better than men do now. All these things are plainly possible for him. They pass out of his tormented desire now, they elude and mock him, because chance, confusion and squalor rule his life. All the gifts of destiny are overlaid and lost to him. He must still suspect and fear.

Within the peace and freedom our Open Conspiracy will win, all these good things that escape us now may be ensured. A graver humanity, stronger, more lovely, longer lived, will learn and develop the ever-enlarging possibilities of its destiny. For the first time, the full beauty of this world will be revealed to its unhurried eyes. Its thoughts will be to our thoughts as the thoughts of a man to the troubled mental experimenting of a child. And all the best of us will be living on in that ampler life, as the child and the things it tried and learnt still live in the man. When we were children, we could not think or feel as we think and feel to-day, but to-day we can peer back and still recall something of the ignorances and guesses and wild hopes of these nigh forgotten years. And so mankind, ourselves still living, dispersed and reconstructed in the future, will recall with affection and understanding the desperate wishes and troubled efforts of our present state.

How can we anticipate the habitations and ways, the usages and adventures, the mighty employments, the ever-increasing knowledge and power of the days to come ? No more than a child with its scribbling paper and its box of bricks can picture or model the undertakings of its adult years. Our battle is with cruelties and frustrations, stupid, heavy and hateful things from which we shall escape at last, less like victors conquering a world than like sleepers awaking from a nightmare in the dawn. From any dream, however dismal and horrible, one can escape by realising that it is a dream ; by saying, " I will awake." The Open Conspiracy is the awaking of mankind from a nightmare of the struggle for existence and the inevitability of war. The light of day thrusts between our eyelids and the multitudinous sounds of morning clamour in our ears. A time will come when men will sit with history before them or with some old newspaper before them, and ask incredulously, " Was there ever such a world ? "

NOTE ON THE MARGIN OF THESE BLUE PRINTS

Such is the truth of human possibility and our necessities as I perceive it, and that is the way man must live if our species is to survive and pass on to greater destinies. I set down the truth as it is given me to see it ; for me there can be no other truth. On every hand about us all is the darkness of the unknown, but the light we have, when we have used our eyes to their utmost, must be our guide. Because of obtuseness and prepossessions, I may but run beside the realities I imagine I express. Necessarily reality which goes on all over the universe and for every instant of time, is infinitely more intricate and wonderful than any statement, teeming with possibilities still unsuspected. All the more do we need compass and map and plans to keep our direction through the jungle of its manifest marvels and dangers. That this presentation of the current phase of human life as the occasion for an Open Conspiracy to establish a world commonweal will seem to many an extreme simplification of our circumstances, should not condemn it. The value of a map lies in the fact that it is not a model nor a picture of reality but a reduced abstraction, sufficiently clear and sufficiently true to essentials and sufficiently free from irrelevancies to guide.

This scheme to thrust forward and establish a human control over the destinies of life and liberate it from its present dangers, uncertainties and miseries, is offered here as an altogether practicable one, subject only to one qualification, that sufficient men and women will be willing to serve it. That there is no foretelling. It is clear that the whole growth is dependent upon the appearance of those primary groups, sustaining and spreading its fundamental ideas. Those ideas have to become the mental substratum of constructive effort. If those ideas can find sufficient vigorous, able and devoted people for their establishment, the rest will follow. There is need of much leadership, not indeed the leadership of a single leader, for the days of spiritual monarchies are over, nor for the leadership of exaggerated figureheads, but for the energetic initiatives of many co-operating personalities. I will not speculate where these leaders are now, in universities, in laboratories, in studies, in factories, in mines, in technical schools, but I have a firm belief that they will come to the call of our mighty opportunities.

For my generation, the rôle of John the Baptist must be our extreme ambition. We can proclaim and make evident the advent of a new phase of human faith and effort. We can point out the path it has been our lifework to discover. We have struggled through the thought and bitter experiences of our time. We have hammered out our instinctive individualism on the anvil of socialism ; we have witnessed the apocalypse of the Great War ; we have been misled, we have stumbled through depths of despair, we have learnt. " Here," we say, " is what we have made of it all. Here is the basis for a new world." In the few years remaining to us we can hope to do no more than that. It is for you to say whether you will set your feet in this direction and go along with us and go further. Upon you—individually and multitudinously—the future rests. Here and there chance may correct and supplement the efforts of our race and save us from the full penalties of our mistakes and negligencies, but saving the impact of some unimagined disaster from outer space, the ultimate decision of the fate of life upon this planet lies now in the will of man.

THE END

CPSIA information can be obtained
at www.ICGtesting.com
Printed in the USA
BVHW03s0611200818
R8957900001B/R89579PG524261BVX12B/1/P